lesley a. northup

ituality **patterns of spirituality** *patterns of spirituali*
atterns of spirituality patterns of spirituality patterns
f spirituality patterns of spirituality patterns of spirit
uality patterns of spirituality patterns of spirituality p

ritualizing
women

The Pilgrim Press   *Cleveland, Ohio*

The Pilgrim Press, Cleveland, Ohio 44115
© 1997 by Lesley A. Northup

Some of the material in this book appeared previously in my articles "Claiming Horizontal Space: Women's Religious Rituals," *Studia Liturgica* 25, no. 1 (1995); "Emerging Patterns in Women's Ritualizing," *Journal of Ritual Studies* 9, no. 2 (summer 1996); and "Narrative in Women's Ritualizing," *Women and Language* 14, no. 1 (spring 1996). I am grateful to the editors of these journals for permission to republish these materials here.

Biblical quotations are from the New Revised Standard Version of the Bible, © 1989 by the Division of Christian Education of the National Council of the Churches of Christ in the U.S.A., and are used by permission.

02 01 00 99 98 97   5 4 3 2 1

Library of Congress Cataloging-in-Publication Data
Northup, Lesley A.
    Ritualizing women : patterns of spirituality / Lesley A. Northup.
        p. cm.
    Includes bibliographical references and index.
    ISBN 0-8298-1213-X (alk. paper)
    1. Women and religion—North America. 2. Women—Religious life—North America. 3. Public worship. 4. Rites and ceremonies—North America. 5. Feminist theology—North America. 6. Feminism—Religious aspects. I. Title.
BL458.N67   1997
291.3'8'082—dc21   97-31512
                                                                   CIP

for dayle

contents

introduction introduction **introduction** *introduction introduction introduction introduction introduction introduction introduction introduction introduction introduction*

This book is about what women do when they get together to worship. Recorded history provides only rare glimpses of women's religious rituals. Although we know that various early, preliterate cultures honored female deities and accorded much freedom to women, little evidence of their ritual patterns has survived, and we can only speculate on the role of women in their worship.[1] Since those ancient days, seldom have women had the opportunity (or, perhaps, the inclination) to worship independently of men. When they have—as, for example, in the practice of witchcraft, in the women's societies of West Africa, or in Roman Catholic and Anglican women's religious orders—their ritual activities have often been necessarily private and unrecorded. Margaret Thompson Drewal, speaking of the Yoruba in Africa, comments:

> Women organize spectacles too, but they tend to be more localized within individual compounds and do not attract men like men's spectacles seem to attract women. By the same token, there are more restrictions placed on women in performances organized by men than there seem to be on men in women's performances. Why?
>
> I have pursued this question with male ritual specialists in Yoruba areas. . . . They invariably have told me that women are much more secretive and exclusive than men are. Women, however, do not seem to be as preoccupied with the idea of secrecy as are men, and in a curious way this makes women appear all the more secretive.[2]

1

Alternatively, women's rituals have been overlooked or dismissed by male observers, as in this statement from a fairly recent study of Australian aboriginal practices:

> Aboriginal women have ceremonies of their own, some commemorating their 'femaleness,' some with highly erotic content, but little is known of these except that they seem to be a pale imitation of masculine ceremonies and they play little part in tribal life.[3]

The reasons for this scholarly disdain are listed by Marjorie Procter-Smith:

> fear and antipathy toward the female body; assumptions of male domination and female subservience as divinely ordained and/or modeled; protocols of prayer adopted from imperial court protocols; the dichotomy of public and private; hierarchical male images and names for God; and [for Christians] the significance attached to the maleness of Jesus.[4]

Despite such difficulties, women as women continue to worship together throughout the world. Some pockets of women's worship remain as variations on older religions, whereas newer groups have evolved in response to the insights of the women's movement, feminist research, the decline of Christendom, and the revival of pagan practices. Consequently, recent years have witnessed a rapidly expanding interest in the ways that women, left to their own devices, develop religious ritual.

A few so-called traditional religions (or ritual subunits of religions), such as those documented by anthropologist Susan Starr Sered in her recent study *Priestess, Mother, Sacred Sister*, offer expansive roles to women. Sered's example religions vary substantially in the degree of control and freedom they afford women and in the relative levels of participation of men and women. Nonetheless, Sered offers compelling evidence that women's worship is distinctive and that many of its elements cross geographic and cultural boundaries.[5]

The range of this comparative similitude is evident in Sered's inclusion of "feminist spirituality" as a woman-dominated religion.[6] In the West, many Jewish and Christian women, finding a lack of widespread support for even such conservative goals as integrating women into existing liturgies through ordination, imaginative biblical interpretation, and the use of expansive language in ritual texts, have formed themselves into ritualizing groups—Christian, Jewish, pagan, feminist, and/ or nontheistic—that seek a unique women's spirituality.

Sered outlines three cultural factors that tend to be associated with the development of women's religions: matrifocality, changing notions of gender, and a high degree of autonomy for women. Western cultures, particularly (but not only) in North America, are gradually but dramatically evidencing not one but two of these factors, as attitudes toward gender change and women gain increasing self-determination. It is hardly surprising, then, that in these societies, women have been able to find, at least to some degree, the freedom to meet, to explore alternatives, to create meaningful ritual patterns, and to worship in accordance with them.

This book focuses specifically (though not exclusively) on those women's religious communities that have self-consciously and intentionally tried to establish comfortable and meaningful patterns of worship. Perforce, this results in an emphasis on the insights of contemporary Western women's groups, feminist and otherwise. Not only do today's women's groups display a degree of intentionality that highlights those elements that arise out of their gendered experience, but because women in these communities have developed ritual patterns deliberately divorced from patriarchal assumptions, what they seek to find, develop, and reclaim is perhaps more useful in identifying what works for women than are evolving ancient rituals bound by cultural norms that limit women's expression. In this sense, modern Western women's ritualizing may offer a kind of stripped-down core view of what many worshiping women do when they choose, rather than inherit, what to do. Moreover, practically speaking, more data is available on such groups, as they become increasingly visible, than on more isolated cultures. Finally, quite frankly, since my own research has been largely in North American ritual studies, these are the religious practices with which I am most familiar. Despite this emphasis, however, I have, where appropriate, integrated examples to illustrate the applicability of these observations to other cultures and practices.

The proposition that there is such a thing as women's ritualizing cannot be advanced without a cautionary word. Certainly, in this postmodern era, many would argue against the making of any universal claims for women's experience, including women's worship. Feminist thought has undergone a rapid evolution on this issue and is hardly monolithic. Caroline Walker Bynum notes that feminist interests shifted from an emphasis in the early 1970s on the similarities between men and women to a stress on their differences—and women's uniqueness—in the early 1980s.[7] In the 1990s, however, some poststructural theorists have rejected altogether the notion of what has been called the "romantic Universal Women's Culture kind of construction." Mary McClintock Fulkerson, expressing a contemporary concern, challenges the politics of identity that assumes that "something is common to or shared universally by all women" or that there is such a thing as "women's experience."[8] Indeed, notes Esther Reed, "postmodernism threatens to erase the unified category 'woman'" altogether.[9]

This concern about essentialism reflects a growing awareness that the experiences of women are individually rooted in each one's culture, time, and circumstances. As Denise J. J. Dijk writes from the Netherlands, "There are no universally valid images of the relationship between God and women. Re-imagining expresses experiences and expectations that are specific for each individual woman."[10]

Among feminist authors, this view is increasingly influential. As recently as 1993, Marjorie Procter-Smith wrote that "it is possible to universalize from women's experience."[11] Her more recent work, however, indicates that she may be developing a different approach. The introduction to Carol P. Christ and Judith Plaskow's popular 1979 anthology *Womanspirit Rising* includes a subchapter titled "Two Views of Women's Experience," in which women's experience is assumed to be a unitary category; their subsequent 1989 book *Weaving the Visions* makes a point of renouncing the term on the grounds that it was created by white, middle-class women who overgeneralized their own experience. Nonetheless, even though Christ and Plaskow acknowledged the need to recognize difference, they concluded that the category "women's experience" was still valid.[12]

Other feminists, although recognizing the demands of difference, particularity, and multiplicity, are wary of the poststructuralist approach, on the grounds that, among other things, it would seem to mute any appeal to a politics of oppression.[13] Moreover, carried to its logical extreme, the particularist approach would eventually make it impossible to perform any meaningful analysis of a subject. Indeed, although many feminists now reject the category "women's experience," or even "women," they apparently remain comfortable with the term "feminist," which refers to a phenomenon at least equally diffuse.

Despite the postmodernist movement, a number of scholars not only assume that there is such a thing as women's experience, but specifically relate it to ritual activity. Nancy Auer Falk and Rita M. Gross, for example, discuss the "common patterns of women's religious lives" and "the many rites and ceremonies that women celebrate on their own," practices that "reflect women's most common concerns and experiences."[14] Bynum not only affirms the category of women's experience but also delineates women's distinctive use of symbols (and consequently, of ritual):

> Women's mode of using symbols seems given to the muting of opposition, whether through paradox or through synthesis; men's mode seems characterized by emphasis on opposition, contradiction, inversion, and conversion. Women's myths and rituals tend to explore a state of being; men's tend to build elaborate and discrete stages between self and other.[15]

Even Fulkerson admits that there are some contexts in which it may be valid to speak of women's experience—for example, "within the context of a women's consciousness-raising group or other interpersonal setting."[16] This is precisely the location of women's intentional religious groups, both contemporary and, often, traditional. The key here is intentionality; the self-conscious quality of communities formed by women to allow worship as women encourages the use of elements that express, across a variety of cultural particularities, not only women's experience but also women's feelings, needs, yearnings, and aesthetics.

Much the same contention is made by Sered, who finds several common themes in the religions she identifies as dominated by and oriented toward women—among them emphases on motherhood, on suffering, on reverence for ancestors, and on interpersonal relationships. Early in her study, she clarifies that "gender has a significant—although not absolute or universal—impact on . . . the form and interpretation of the rituals performed."[17] She notes that even if we cannot overgeneralize about women, there are relevant social patterns that may be, if not common to all women, common among women in particular cultures. Yet she concludes that her somewhat arbitrarily chosen religions have "more in common with men's religions of the same time and place than with women's religions located on different continents," attributing this largely to "dissimilar histories of the women's religions."[18]

Sered's obvious difficulty in trying to reconcile the competing claims of commonality and particularity arises in part, perhaps, because of her reliance on data from religions or ritual subunits of religions that are still partially under male control. These religions largely either "exist in a society where the dominant religion is male dominated, . . . co-exist alongside of, and sometimes intertwined with, male-dominated religions . . . [or] are sects of otherwise male-dominated religions."[19] Only in the Ryukyu Islands and Belize is woman-dominated religion primary, and both cultures are otherwise clearly patriarchal.

Of course, the same can be said for Western cultures—women's religious activity in Europe and North America obviously is situated in cultures that are principally male-oriented. Yet a difference can be noted between the newer and older versions of women's religion. Although the religions Sered discusses are dominated primarily by women, much of that mastery is ceded conditionally by men, and women must still in many ways conform to the tradition from which they evolved or to male power brokers behind the scenes. Thus, although these religions evidence many of the elements common to women's spiritual communities, other typical elements may have difficulty surfacing because of imposed cultural circumstances, and still others may not appear because women do not really control the group's symbolic expression. In contrast, Western women are increasingly claiming a kind of religious independence not often found elsewhere and hard enough to achieve here.

A researcher trying to chart the course of women's ritualizing must somehow overcome several major obstacles. First is a definitional problem. No one is sure just what we're talking about. Most of the literature to date—and there's not much of it—focuses on feminist liturgy. But to look at this phenomenon clearly, we have to see beyond the large feminist tail that at the moment is wagging the dog and consider other instances of women intentionally gathering together, either in concert with or in opposition to the prevailing religious system, to worship as women.

A second problem is that, especially in its most modern phase, women's ritualizing has quite deliberately not left a paper trail. Given the postmodern assumptions of feminist worship, each liturgical event is understood as an expression of the particularity of the group engaged in it; it is flexible and adaptable to its time, place, and circumstances, and thus it is not reproducible. Consequently, although certain patterns have emerged as common to women's liturgies, there is little textual material extant.

Finally, it would be helpful if we could derive some sort of time line of the critical moments in the development of women's ritualizing, but that, too, is shrouded in a haze of particularity, much like the trees that obscure the view of the forest. In its contemporary manifestation, the movement toward women's worship has no central trunk; rather, it has evolved as random branches, with no coordination, from the discontents and yearnings of women, in one small group after another. Many of these branches bloom briefly, then soon wither. Others shift and change and merge. Few keep or publish records. Probably the closest thing to a seriously organized movement is Women-church, which is coordinated in a nonrestrictive way. Although I attempt in chapter 1 to highlight some moments along the path of the development of women's ritualization, a more definitive history remains elusive.

The source materials for this project are considerably more varied than is typical of a scholarly work. Principally, they include relevant scholarship from such diverse fields as ritual studies, anthropology, history, theology, feminist theory, liturgics, sociology, and cultural criticism. Somewhere at the center of this tangled web of intersecting disciplines lies the study of women's ritualizing. But it would be breaking faith with the subject of the book to exclude accounts of the actual experiences of worshiping women, as expressed in more popular literature, in reports on ritualizing events, in works promoting women's spirituality, in interviews, and in my own observations. There is also a growing body of practical writings suggesting texts or outlines for women's rituals. These, too, have a place in this book.

As this amalgam suggests, there are several things this book is not. First, as I have indicated, this book is not a feminist tract; although feminist insights are critical to even the most rudimentary study of women's ritualizing, and although feminist worship communities provide excellent laboratories for understanding this phenomenon, I have tried to go beyond the specifics of feminist liturgics to make connections with the ways that women in other contexts ritualize. I am trying to broaden the discussion to "women," rather than "feminists," insofar as it is responsibly possible to use such categories. I have also sought to expand the topic beyond liturgics to the more inclusive perspective of ritual studies.

This book is also not an anthropological, ethnographic, or phenomenological study. It does not focus on one particular worshiping community, nor does it fully document the variety of women's ritualizing in all times and all places. It does not "do" theology or philosophy, or provide a ritual studies hermeneutics. Indeed, it does not offer any systematic interpretation of its subject. Neither is it primarily a theoretical work. Rather, it seeks to be descriptive, analytic, and suggestive.

The ritual events cited were chosen on the basis of their value as illustrations, and they cover a broad range of activities. Traditional religions, distinct communities within some of those religions, and alternative religions, in addition to contemporary women's worship, provide important insights. Some of these groups have been successful, in the sense that they have continued on in time; others have not. It is my conviction, however, that they all demand consideration as this genre starts to define itself. In using them, I have tried to bear in mind John Hilary Martin's warning that "comparisons between isolated fragments of religious material . . . are of dubious validity at best";[20] consequently, I have tried to limit examples to religious groups about which sufficient information exists to be able to say something substantive.

Chapter 1 outlines the sources and contexts of women's ritualizing, provides a brief summary of the development of modern women's spirituality, and clarifies terminology. Chapter 2 delineates the perhaps controversial contention that women's ritualizing uses similar ritual elements, in varying combinations, regardless of where it occurs. Chapter 3 addresses the issue of ritual space and time and their reconceptualization by worshiping women. Chapter 4 discusses the role of narrative in women's ritualizing and reflects on the impact of cultural criticism on how women use biography and story. Chapter 5 examines the relationship of politics and women's spirituality, investigating ritual functions and outcomes. Chapter 5 considers whether women's ritualizing constitutes a legitimate subfield of ritual studies and looks at some of the challenges that arise as women's spirituality moves into the twenty-first century.

Rollo May has written that "what has been lacking in our modern culture are myths and rituals to give significance to the woman's life apart from what she has in relation to man."[21] In this book, I attempt to outline some common patterns of the new ritualizing that is responding to that concern. I make no claim either that contemporary or earlier women's ritualizing is common to all women or that its images and practices are unique to women. Indeed, some male-dominated religions incorporate elements commonly found when women worship, and many women—the vast majority, in fact—worship comfortably in those religions. I intend not to denigrate the vast body of ritual activity in which both men and women participate, nor to claim that all women worship in the same way, but to identify and reflect upon the nature of ritual designed and enacted by women when they do set themselves apart.

My hope is that this book will not so much provide answers as raise provocative questions, not the least of which is whether women's ritualizing can be considered a distinct subgenre of ritual studies or liturgics. More generally, I hope that, sparking discussion and heightening awareness, it will begin to outline a subject that has been dealt with heretofore only peripherally or in article-length publications. Perhaps it might encourage more women to explore ritualizing possibilities and help legitimate their efforts.

ritualizing **defining women's ritualizing** *definin women's ritualizing defining women's ritualizing de-fining women's ritualizing defining women's ritualizi*

Not long ago, someone circulated a cartoon that pictured an ancient sacrificial rite. There, supine on a great stone altar, a young woman lay waiting for the strike of a great knife held poised over her chest by an elaborately vested priest. One onlooker commented to another, "Serves her right. She was always whining about women not being allowed to participate in the services."

Recent years have witnessed a rapidly expanding interest in the variety of ways that women seek to participate in religious ritual. For a few women in some less familiar religions in various corners of the world, this is not an issue: they already lead and fully participate in their ritual communities. In the biblical religions, however, debate has centered on such matters as ordination, scriptural interpretation, and the use of expansive language in ritual texts. For women committed to remaining in those traditional institutions, the issues have largely involved just what position women will assume vis-à-vis the altar (or *bima*). Still other women are seeking religious meaning in deliberately women-centered spirituality, in which they are actively engaged in creative ritualizing.

Locating Women's Ritualizing

Defining women's ritualizing can be problematic, not least because women ritualize in a wide variety of contexts and patterns. Women can be found worshiping together both within institutional religions and consciously divorced from them; singly and in community; domestically and in public; in classical forms and innovatively.

Anthropologist Susan Starr Sered has documented a number of religions—often sects or subunits of what we think of as the world's "great" religions—founded, led, populated by, or otherwise "dominated" by women. These groups include Afro-Brazilian sects, Christian Science, Korean shamanism, Islamic zar cults, Shakerism, northern Thai matrilineal spirit cults, Ryukyuan Island religion, Burmese nat cults, and American Spiritualism. Other candidates for a list of women's religions include the "auxiliary examples" noted, but not discussed, by Sered (for example, the Beguines, American Vodou, and Japanese Tensho-Kotai-Jingukyo) and a number of the groups investigated by the authors in Catherine Wessinger's edited collection *Women's Leadership in Marginal Religions,* which concentrates on U.S. religions.[1]

Clearly, women do manage to get together for worship of their own design, even within religions and cultures otherwise dominated by men. In the post-Christian West, this phenomenon has emerged in the form of a grassroots movement to create women's spirituality groups, usually focused on ritual activity. Such groups include women disaffected with traditional religion, politically attuned feminists, unchurched women looking for a meaningful spiritual experience, former New Age seekers, and women of all classes and ethnicities looking for safe and affirming community. Their gatherings take a variety of forms. Charlotte Caron lists four: Christian feminists, women-church, goddess spirituality, and consciousness-raising groups.[2]

As a delineation of women's ritualizing groups, this schema needs some revision. For one thing, Christian feminists (and Jewish feminists and, for that matter, feminists within other institutional religions) remain, by Caron's definition, within the ritual structure of their religions, rather than forming distinct ritualizing groups. They generally believe in working for reform from within, participating in traditional liturgies, and exerting pressure for the fuller inclusion of women and women's concerns in ritual practice.

Caron's view that Christian feminists do not create separate ritualizing groups is echoed by Cynthia Eller, who justifies her exclusion of Christian women from the category of feminist spirituality on the grounds that Christian feminists criticize, then leave, their religions.[3] Despite this analysis, one of the most widespread and visible communities of the movement is Women-church, a loose convergence spearheaded primarily by Roman Catholic women, most of whom still claim allegiance to their church. Women-church blossomed from a seed planted over a decade ago, when Rosemary Radford Ruether drew the outline of a new forum for women's spirituality. The movement has grown rapidly; there are now even national Women-church conferences. In Women-church, as Ruether puts it, "women have begun to take the shaping of the symbolic universe of meaning into their own hands."[4] A similar phenomenon is occurring among Jewish feminists.

A third way that women have reorganized themselves spiritually is in reclaiming the ancient worship of the goddess. Many women have decided that only the contemplation of a female deity can resonate with their spiritual intuition, though it is hardly true that "almost all spiritual feminists" focus on the goddess, as Eller has it.[5] Goddess religion is implicitly traditional, seeking to recover beliefs and practices that predated the Semitic religions. Carol P. Christ and Judith Plaskow warn that reconstructions of goddess worship risk failing to make a great enough break with the past while simultaneously romanticizing it.[6]

Another stream of feminist practice is Wicca. Caron too easily conflates goddess spirituality with feminist Wicca, although they are distinct—albeit sometimes intertwined—women's religious movements. Indeed, as the witch Starhawk insists, "Feminist spirituality, Paganism, and Witchcraft overlap but are not identical communities."[7] Wiccans often are not exclusively intent on a female deity, nor do they consistently consider their traditional roots to be identical with those of goddess religions. Although both groups share a deep grounding in the power and sacredness of nature, the ritual practice of "the craft," with its frequent focus on magic, often differs radically from that of goddess worship. Moreover, not all Wiccans are feminist.

Caron's fourth category, consciousness-raising groups, incorporates elements of spirituality that arise out of a sense of women's community. Study gatherings, literary discussion circles, activist organizations, and even traditional "women's auxiliary" groups can become the core of a feminist experiential community that perceives a spiritual dimension in its shared life. Because Caron eschews New Age spirituality, she would probably not include the feminist groups arising on what ritologist Ronald Grimes calls the "workshop circuit" that wends its way through alternative institutions such as Esalen and Naropa. As Grimes notes, however, many of these groups are feminist.[8] Perhaps such New Age feminists should constitute their own category.

Contemporary Women's Ritualizing, Briefly

No fixed date marks the start of the movement toward women's spirituality gatherings in the West. The United States, in particular, has provided fertile ground for women's societies of one sort or another that have worshiped independently of male control. By the 1740s, for example, American Moravians had established separate communal living arrangements for married members, single men, and single women. The diary of the single sisters' "choir" testifies to its independent worship, a practice that in some locations tended to near-fanatical devotion to Jesus as spouse.[9]

Women also gathered together for worship in the missionary societies that flourished around the turn of the century in the Episcopal, Roman Catholic, and Methodist churches, among others. Similarly, organizations such as the Women's Christian Temperance Union (WCTU), the Salvation Army and Church Army, parochial women's auxiliaries, and deaconess houses developed distinctive worship practices in their heyday. Of course, Roman Catholic and Anglican women's religious orders had long practiced conventual piety and discretionary liturgies, providing a model that, although it was not always consciously appropriated by the organizers of women's communities, nonetheless stood as silent witness to the ritual feasibility of such groups.

The current movement developed in tandem with what started as women's liberation and evolved into feminism. In particular, it seems to be an outgrowth of the boom in feminist theology in the 1970s and 1980s. The publication of seemingly prophetic works—such as Valerie Saiving's 1960 article "The Human Situation: A Feminine View," Rosemary Lauer's 1963 article "Women and the Church" in *Commonweal,* and, in the wake of Vatican II in 1968, Mary Daly's *The Church and the Second Sex*—began to focus women's perceptions that they were not getting a fair shake in their traditional religions.[10]

The 1970s witnessed the release of a number of feminist theological texts, as Rosemary Radford Ruether and others began to question their Christian and Jewish heritages seriously. On another level, women were meeting in consciousness-raising groups and other discussion forums, in some cases discovering the roots of sexism in religion. By 1975, Daly had already declared herself a "postchristian feminist," and her dramatic and very public departure from the church spotlighted questions about the extent to which women were, could be, and ought to be part of traditional religions.[11] The mid-1970s was probably the critical period during which it began to occur to women in significant, if not large, numbers that there were alternatives—some that allowed remaining in the institutional church, others that required leave-taking.

At the same time, women's (and later, feminist) scholarship was uncovering a variety of resources that helped educate people in general about attitudes of the church toward women, the possibility that women had taken a more active role in the early church than was assumed, and the accomplishments of the first wave of suffragists and other feminists who had altered American society and produced such works as the *Woman's Bible*. Courses on women and religion sprang up, and otherwise isolated women began to sense that something bound them together. As Daly noted in her preface to the 1985 reissue of *The Church and the Second Sex*, she, like many other women, had discovered a powerful new community—a community of like-minded women.[12]

This idea took shape in the ad hoc, local formation of women's groups that met to discuss their frustrations with religious institutions, their unmet spiritual needs, and the possibility of doing things differently. Although most of these did not come to light until some years later, feminist movement media sources such as *WomanSpirit*, *Quest*, and the interestingly named *Lady-Unique-Inclination-of-the-Night* had been documenting ritual practices among women since 1974.[13] In 1974, Arlene Swidler published the first collection of women's rituals (a rarity in the ad hoc world of feminist texts), rituals that acknowledged Christian, Jewish, ecumenical, pagan, and other root sources.[14] Although the strongest ferment seemed to occur, as might be expected, in urban areas, as early as 1980 there was a feminist spiritual community in, of all places, Portland, Maine, and, still further afield, a Saskatchewan Christian Feminist Network.[15] The Women's Liturgy Group of New York City, begun in 1981 by a small group of Catholic women, quickly grew to the point that a split into two groups proved necessary.

While Christian and Jewish women were sorting out their relationships with their respective religious institutions and rituals, other women, having completely given up or having never been active in a Western religion, were rediscovering the fact that many early religions focused on a female deity. By the early 1970s, pagan groups were already flourishing—most including both men and women—in San Francisco and elsewhere. These groups attempted to recover or imaginatively reconstruct ancient ceremonies that reverenced the earth and forces of nature, that incorporated the use of herbs and natural remedies, and that gave equal or even preferential status to women and female deities.

In 1976, the witch Starhawk formed the Covenant of the Goddess, an outgrowth of the Bay Area Witches. By this time, many Wiccan and pagan groups had started to focus on the goddess as a symbol of the sustaining divine presence. Daly's appropriation of words such as "witch" and "crone" as complementary to women in her 1978 *Gyn/Ecology* furthered the connection between feminism and neopaganism that had first surfaced with the New York political collective WITCH in the late 1960s.[16] The liturgical life of these witches and pagans evidenced a surprising confluence of elements that were also emerging in the developing Christian and Jewish women's groups.

The evolution of these various groups was obviously a grassroots movement: they had no central organization, no hierarchy of leadership, no effective means of widespread communication, no evangelistic imperatives. They just started happening all over as women in different places came to similar recognitions. Nor was their development smooth or painless. As one group member reported,

> Early on, rituals tended to be self-conscious or timid, overly or underly programmed. Since the group was not adhering to a text, some were thematically programmed. The use of objects often lacked real symbolic resonance; selected texts were frequently either too cerebral or too poetic to elicit an authentic response.[17]

The movement at this stage was principally a North American phenomenon. Nonetheless, the resemblance of this process to the growth of basic ecclesial communities (BECs) in Latin America was not lost on many women, especially those from Roman Catholic backgrounds. Indeed, BECs, some formed as long ago as the 1950s, in many cases have provided a model for the grassroots development of faith and praxis that is at the heart of women's ritualizing, even for women who no longer consider themselves Christian.[18]

Perhaps the best-known and most influential—certainly the most organized—of these women's communities is Women-church, a network of groups that have taken the name of Ruether's groundbreaking 1985 book *Women-Church*. In it, Ruether outlined what she saw as a "feminist religious revolution" whose shape was still unclear, and she outlined some possible ritual directions for the movement. Ruether contended that "the creation of liturgy is properly a function of local communities who are engaged in a collective project woven from the fabric of many concrete stories that make up the lives of each member of that body."[19] This sounds not unlike the outlook of BECs. Ruether credits

BECs as major influences on the development of the movement, along with several other forces: the renewal of women's religious orders after Vatican II, the increasing number of Christian churches ordaining women, the impact of liberation theology and feminism, and the rising number of women attending seminaries.[20] Her claim that "Women-church represents the first time that women collectively have claimed to be church"[21] is sweeping but perhaps true in the somewhat limited context of traditional Christianity.

In 1983, a plurality of Catholic women's groups, including the National Coalition of American Nuns (whose members, after all, had long been doing all-women's liturgies), WATER (the Women's Alliance for Theology, Ethics, and Ritual), the Women's Ordination Conference (WOC), and several others, formed the Women of the Church Coalition. Its 1983 conference succeeded the WOC conferences of 1975 and 1979 and was "the first effort to define and collectively experience a new stance toward being feminists in exodus within the church."[22] The small number of Protestants present ensured that the movement would be ecumenical, although it remains largely Roman Catholic. The second meeting, in 1987, was attended by more than three thousand and began to attract institutional opposition.[23] Women-church has now become truly international, with groups around the world.

Concurrently, ecumenical groups have developed in Europe and elsewhere. Denise J. J. Dijk reports that feminist services were being held in the Netherlands as early as the 1970s and were expanded dramatically in the early 1980s. The first major conference on feminism and liturgy was held there in 1985, and a women's information center on liturgy was established.[24] In England, women's groups started coming together after 1978, when the Church of England failed to vote in favor of women's ordination. These communities now include the well-known St. Hilda Community, the Catholic Women's Network, the Movement for the Ordination of Women, the Oxford Women's Liturgy Group, CHLOE'S People (Creative Happenings, Liturgy, and Other Events), and Women in Theology.[25] Moreover, Women-church continues to provide communications channels for women from Australia to Africa to South America, enabling women in disparate cultures to consider the possibilities of women's worship.

As women's groups have found, religious conferences turn out to be largely liturgical. The core nature of liturgical ritual in forming and shaping the identity of a religious community clearly cannot be escaped.

Even when women meet ostensibly to discuss matters of faith or discouragement with patriarchy, in short order their gatherings turn to questions of how to express that faith in symbols and metaphors that affirm their own experience.

Nowhere was this more evident—and more criticized—than at the Re-Imagining Conference sponsored by a number of mainline churches and held in November 1993 in Minneapolis. The event was meant to be a creative gathering for both women and men and included a variety of presentations, meetings, discussions, and entertainment. But virtually all that the press reported was the liturgies, which inserted into this mainstream format images and ritual elements common to women's ritualizing groups. The conference was a smashing success in Minneapolis, less so in the Christian community at large. Some traditionalists were upset by intercessory language evoking such images as the "nectar between our thighs [with which] we invite a lover, we birth a child." Still, the conference spurred increased awareness of the extent and attraction of the movement, with a consequent rise in scholarly as well as ecclesiastical interest. As an epilogue to the conference, religious women have created a growing support and information network with its own journal, *Reimagining*.

A Note on Women's Renewal and Liturgical Renewal

This discussion raises the intriguing question of the relationship of women's ritualizing to the liturgical movement that peaked in the 1960s and 1970s. Certainly, some of the same principles emerged in that earlier movement. These are evident in the church architecture of the period, with its extensive use of circular and semicircular designs; in the substantial changes in ritual postures and movements that accompanied the adoption of new texts; and in the growing theology of shared ritual leadership that resulted in the heightened involvement of the laity in liturgical ministry.

Although both movements have progressed toward a communal model, there seems to be little evidence of a direct link between the liturgical renewal movement and women's renewal. Indeed, as Mary Collins notes, "I would be hard pressed to show the presence of strong feminist consciousness in this process of liturgical change, even in 1993."[26] Few women were early leaders in both spheres, though in later years prominent feminist liturgiologists have emerged. Few male liturgical experts, who largely remain representatives of their traditions, have recognized a correspondence between women's issues and liturgical theology.

Marjorie Procter-Smith has noted several clear distinctions between the two movements. Among these disconnections are the liturgical movement's focus on reclaiming old texts and practices—an interest not shared by Christian, Jewish, and post-Christian women, though evident in the development of some pagan and Wiccan groups. She also notes the sharp difference in the relative level of acceptance encountered by both movements, crediting the success of liturgical renewal to the power and authority of its male leaders, whereas women's independent worship has faced resistance in many quarters. Despite these concerns, Procter-Smith nonetheless concludes that the two movements share common ground and the possibility of fruitful dialogue.[27]

Nonetheless, pending further research, the only clear connection of the two movements is a common grounding in the zeitgeist of egalitarian renewal and reform. It may be safe to speculate, however, that the apparent end—or plateau—of the liturgical reform era has spurred women who despair of further change within the churches to seek spiritual fulfillment in other venues.

Women's Ritualizing and Feminist Ritualizing

Most of the authors writing today on women and religious ritual—Procter-Smith, Eller, Caron, and Starhawk, to name but a few—write from a feminist perspective. This is hardly surprising, considering the close link between the rise of feminist consciousness and the development of women's spirituality groups. Moreover, the majority of these communities are unquestionably feminist. A feminist viewpoint includes, in most of these writings and groups, a political as well as a spiritual commitment to substantial cultural transformation, especially for non-white women, women in oppressive societies, and socioeconomically disadvantaged women.

Feminism, however, is not a monolithic body of thought. Feminists come in a variety of flavors. Marianne Ferguson, for instance, divides religious feminists into radical, reconstructionist, and reformist categories.[28] Radical feminists, she suggests, reject conventional religions and are drawn to goddess religions. Reconstructionists are interested in recovering women's experience in scripture and history. Reformist feminists use South America's liberation theologians as a model, reinterpreting the texts and precepts of their religions to argue for an end to oppression and patriarchy. Although this is only one of a number of possible models for understanding the complexity of contemporary religious feminism, it highlights the diversity of feminist approaches to religion and the dangers of a facile identification of women's worship with feminist worship.

Moreover, not all participants in women's ritual gatherings, even in the West, identify themselves as feminist. Some may simply rejoice in the freedom of all-woman worship; others may be looking for a way to correlate their faith with their personal experience. Women in non-Western religions generally do not place feminist issues at the heart of their worship, at least not consciously.

Theresa Berger, a German feminist, is one of the few scholars to acknowledge the broader context of women's ritualizing. Berger eschews the phrase "feminist spirituality" in favor of the more inclusive and perhaps more accurate term "women's liturgical movement."[29] If the study of how women ritualize is to be a legitimate field of inquiry, it must expand beyond the narrower category of feminist ritual to embrace the more complex data provided by the wide range of women who join together in various places and for various reasons to form a ritualizing community. Contemporary ritualizing—often but not always feminist—can provide a paradigm for the development of women's worship groups elsewhere, offering an intensive vision of how women ritualize; but we must guard against mistaking the part for the whole.

Defining Women's Ritualizing

When women gather intentionally to worship, what they are doing is rarely static or passive; most often, it is a vital process, not always successful but always creative—that is, it is ritualizing, rather than observing or participating in a fixed, received ritual. "Ritualizing," as Grimes says, "is the activity of incubating ritual; it is the act of constructing ritual either self-consciously and deliberately or incrementally and editorially."[30] Rebecca Slough writes that ritualizing is a symbiotic process in which "participants bring to the ritual environment social experiences and knowledge outside of that world which are brought to bear upon their actions in the ritual context."[31] Ritualizing—as opposed to "going to mass," "reading the Office," "hearing the Word," "studying Torah," or even formal meditation—is an inventive process that characterizes virtually all the ritual activity attributable specifically to women.

Within Western intentional communities of worshiping women, people are engaged in creative, provocative, and innovative ritualizing: constructing ritual, cultivating attitudes, molding awareness, exploring relationships, and redefining religious practice. As Bridget Rees notes, this creativity may be spontaneous: "Often liturgies have been prepared on the spot using whatever is to hand in terms of experience, symbols, and mood, and always the liturgies arise out of women's experience."[32] But ritualizing also characterizes the ritual activities of women in older religious traditions. Take, for example, the extraliturgical religious activities exercised exclusively by women in some cultures. A complex of images and practices may surface in rituals that, because of their domestic character, are understood to devolve particularly upon women and have thus been left to women to develop and interpret. In one case, Sered writes that "through the process of domestication, women convert male-oriented symbols and rituals to a female-oriented belief system."[33] For the elderly Jewish women she describes, cleaning, candle lighting, and cooking are transformed in the context of the High Holidays into a unique expression of women's spiritual gifts and capabilities. These rituals also provide a platform for solidarity and community among the women who practice them.

Mama Lola, the Vodou woman described in loving detail by Karen McCarthy Brown, confines herself "largely to her house, a place where she is in control."[34] There, in the middle of Brooklyn, she fosters rituals rooted in ancient practice as a builder of altars and a hostess to other worshipers. Her ritual tasks as a priestess are also those of women's domesticity: cooking, healing, singing, nurturing, "helping." The rites she conducts, although open to people of both sexes, are grounded in a network of ritualizing women that begins with the mother-daughter relationship and spirals outward to include other women relatives and friends.[35]

Among the Oglala Sioux, women formerly gathered in ritual sodalities to produce effective war medicine. Their mourning rituals stem from domestic tasks: "A woman's female relatives buy her groceries and deliver them to her home. They also help her by making star quilts, shawls, embroidered towels, pillowcases and sheets." During mourning, women tend the spirit of the deceased, feed it regularly, and accompany it (and each other) about.[36]

In other cultures, marital status, rather than domestic skill, is a more normative determinant of distinctive elements of women's ritualizing.

In parts of Mexico, for example, married women join together to sponsor public masses honoring the Immaculate Conception, in which their virginal daughters process in white; these same adolescent girls form groups to sponsor devotions to St. Theresa. Unmarried women, who are presumed to have excess time, may become "church cockroaches," practically living in the church, interceding for others and attending to the saints.[37]

All this creative ritualizing serves purposes that are both religious and social. "What does ritualization see?" asks Catherine Bell. Her answer:

> It is a way of acting that sees itself as *responding* to a place, event, force, problem, or tradition. It tends to see itself as the natural or appropriate thing to do in the circumstances. Ritualization does not see how . . . its own actions reorder and reinterpret the circumstances so as to afford the sense of a fit among the main spheres of experience—body, community, and cosmos.[38]

Through ritualization, then, women "reorder and reinterpret," converting male-oriented symbols and rituals to a female-oriented belief system.

Ritualizing also provides a platform for solidarity and community among women and for the development of identity; as theologian Tom Driver notes, "It is not as true to say that we human beings invented rituals as that rituals have invented us."[39] Finally, writes Bruce Lincoln, women in oppressive circumstances

> have means—creative and powerful—to react against the processes that victimize them. Among these are the disruption of existing rituals and the creation of novel rituals, to which one might add the critical study of ritual forms, with particular attention to their social contexts and consequences.[40]

It is these disrupting and creative ritual tasks that women's spirituality groups embrace. Because women in such groups are aware that "in many respects the most effective ritual criticism is the development of an alternative rite,"[41] their spirituality groups are demonstrating more interest in generating new rites—that is, in ritualizing—than in finding a place for themselves within old ones. Sered notes that for women in developing rural societies, "the appeal of novel religious groups may lie in the opportunity they offer for the creation of private networks of power, influence and authority in a nondomestic setting."[42] The same is also true for modern Western women. Grimes, remarking that for many women, ritualizing has become perhaps the "primary mode of claiming power to invent, control, and interpret the symbolic resources of their traditions and cultures," asserts that feminist ritual creativity has provided "an ongoing context for ritual experimentation unparalleled in any other sector of North American society."[43]

The task is not without its dangers. Women ritualizing together risk marginalization: "Ritualizing is not often socially supported. Rather, it happens in the margins, on the thresholds; therefore it is alternately stigmatized and eulogized."[44] Certainly, this has been the experience of many women who may already feel marginalized by patriarchal religion. Still, many women have come to assert, along with feminist ethicist Beverly Harrison, that they are "beginning to see the goal to be ritualizing more than ritual."[45]

The Object of Women's Ritualizing

The occasions on which women ritualize are many and varied. In addition to private ritual behaviors, diverse public functions invite ritualizing: women's conferences, award presentations, concerts, craft and skill events, gatherings of professional societies, and a wide range of other organizational activities—as well as times of worship. What distinguishes this last category from the others is, presumably, that it addresses or evokes some object that is not merely utilitarian; something worthy of respect, invocation, or adoration; something evocative of ultimate values; something expressible only through symbol. In other words, in some sense worship is "religious."

This term is notoriously difficult to define, and in the context of women's ritualizing it is so broadly applied that it may often seem barely recognizable to more traditional believers. Most women's spirituality groups continue to struggle with the question of what it is, precisely, to which their worship is directed—what it is that makes them religious. Not much assistance has been forthcoming from observers of the scene. Accordingly, Sered complains that "studies of women and religion are notable for emphasizing ritual instead of theology."[46] Although this situation does not convincingly suggest, as she posits, that researchers and women worshipers simply like ritual more than belief, it does seem plausible that it reflects the relative ease of comparing and analyzing women's ritualizing across varying demographic and cultural factors, whereas the beliefs being ritualized remain flexible, mutational, and hard to correlate.

The object of women's worship, in any event, has not gone unexplored. Feminist theologians have been tackling the question of how to reimage God in Judaism and Christianity since the 1960s, predating any noticeable movement by women toward independent worship. Pagans have reenvisioned the goddess, researching both her ancient and her contemporary qualities. Even those spirituality groups that eschew worship of a recognizable deity revere something—the divinity in nature, in self, or in relatedness.

Notwithstanding caveats about false universals, is it nonetheless possible to identify any common threads in these divergent views of the object of women's worship? Does anything link those women who still talk of "God" with those who can no longer use that language to express the ineffable? The one theme that seems to arise most consistently is that whatever the numinous is, it is immanent rather than transcendent. Worshiping women appear to favor overwhelmingly a vision of indwelling divinity or power, rather than the *ganz andere* described in classic Western theology or the abstraction of being/psyche found in the East. Thus, Ruether talks of Women-church's images of God as "immanentist, female, and relational."[47] Starhawk identifies immanence as one of the three foundational principles of goddess religion, elaborating that "we are each a manifestation of the living being of the earth, [and] that nature, culture, and life in all their diversity are sacred."[48] Mary Farrell Bednarowski expands on this, enumerating some common themes of contemporary women's theology:

> There is an apparent growing preference for Goddess(es) rather than God; an emphasis on divine immanence rather than transcendence; . . . community and interconnectedness over—or at least in addition to—individualism; relationship as an organizational principle rather than hierarchy; self-knowledge or transformation as a worthy goal.[49]

These preferences are not limited to modern feminist spirituality. For example, Theosophy, a century-old religion that scholars generally agree has been dominated by women, is also concerned with the immanence of divinity, an approach that emphasizes a sense of interconnectedness.[50] The same focus on relatedness and inherence characterizes the ancestor reverence of Korean shamanism, the orisha possession of devout followers of various Afro-Caribbean sects, the ecological consciousness of Gaia worship, and the marriage of an Egyptian

Muslim woman to a zar spirit. In fact, these dominant theological features can be identified virtually wherever women gather to worship.[51]

Even the most self-oriented religious systems recognize the need to move beyond the ego; even the most mundane understand the need to focus on larger goals and relationships; even the most independent recognize, invoke, and marshal forces beyond simple mortals. Despite the apparent obscurity of the object of much of women's ritualizing or even the near-atheism of some women's spirituality, at the core is something larger—if only self-discovery through relationship.[52] There would be little point in "religious" ritualizing otherwise.

The Women's Liturgy Group (WLG) of New York, a well-established ecumenical (but largely Roman Catholic) group, still struggles with how to identify the Other:

> WLG has not developed a creed, nor has that been a priority. Members are aware of various ways in which the idea of "god" is being reinterpreted. Although the notion of "goddess" has been introduced from time to time in rituals, the group has not identified exclusively with that or any other image of deity now being scrutinized. Neither, it seems, has the use of the name "God" been examined in depth. However, what the rituals seem to affirm is that, regardless of the restrictions from without, women have access to indwelling spiritual power.[53]

As women seek to identify and come into relationship with that mysterious numinous force, ritual provides the key. Theologian Margaret Farley has said:

> Powerful ritual not only expresses the experiences and the values of those who participate, but also reveals value to them; not only manifests emotional responses that are important to the participants, but also evokes emotional responses; not only rises from the human heart, but also forms the human heart."[54]

Sources for Women's Ritualizing

The power of the creative impulse notwithstanding, all this ritualizing requires raw material from which to construct new ritual patterns. No matter how innovative a group may be, creating rituals from whole cloth is difficult and usually not very satisfying at first. Women have found inspiration for new rituals in a variety of sources.

The Western Liturgical Tradition

Despite what many ritualizing women recognize as the oppressive patriarchy of Western religions, many women are rooted in Christianity or Judaism, which continue to be meaningful ritual resources. Women-church liturgies, for example, often follow familiar Christian formats. Such ritual elements as sharing a loaf of blessed bread, blessing parts of the body with ritual water, or using a greeting of peace are common to both institutional Christian liturgies and new ritualizing communities.

The Rediscovery of Eastern Religion

With the growing influence, since the 1960s, of Asian religious teachings and practices, women have been increasingly exposed to such ritual elements as extended meditation, posture and breathing exercises, chakra concentration, and making mandalas. They have also found useful ritual material in New Age spirituality, which adapts Eastern spiritual techniques (among others) in focusing on personal well-being and the improvement of the self.

Ancient Ritual Traditions

Worshipers of the goddess, midwives, herbal healers, witches, santeras, and visionaries have participated throughout the ages in a unique religious subculture subjected to repression, persecution, and co-optation. Many women's religious groups today draw on sources from this old tradition: oral narratives, surviving ritual patterns, history "read between the lines," rare extant texts. Wiccan practice, for example, is firmly rooted in ritual activities believed to have been passed down through the centuries.

The Rituals of Other Cultures

Although there is considerable discussion about whether the ritual elements of tribal and nontechnological cultures should be mined by modern (mostly white) women, the practices of Native Americans, Africans, tribal cultures, and other societies—especially those that evidence a respect for women and for nature—have inspired much of women's ritualizing.[55]

Natural Patterns, Symbols, and Objects

The use of natural objects and symbols is common to women's spirituality. This is hardly surprising, in light of the traditional equation of women with the forces of nature: female identities have commonly been ascribed to the earth, the sea, and the moon (in some cultures, to the sun as well), and to such natural processes as tropical storms, agricultural productivity, and, of course, human and animal fertility. Although acknowledging the stereotyping that such identifications imply, women are nonetheless particularly attuned to Gaia theology, creation theology, the ecological movement, and their own natural fertility rhythms.

Personal Experience

One of the most significant sources for women's ritualizing, both because of its accessibility and because of its neglect in institutional religions, is the personal experience of women themselves. Women's rituals are often rooted in the lives and activities of women who do housework, produce handicrafts, tolerate abuse, birth and raise children, succeed against all odds in business and professional roles, prepare meals, and survive in community. These activities generate both personal and public ritualizing.

The Women's Movement and Feminist Consciousness

Many women's spirituality groups, although not all, are intentionally feminist: their convictions lead them beyond religious meaning into the politics of justice. For many feminist communities, spiritual strengthening is part of a general concern for empowering women. Feminist insights, writings, and theory often inform women's rituals, provide their thematic content, and inspire women to work for change.

Women's Creativity

Many elements in women's ritualizing arise fresh, newly designed by women using imagination and artistry. Rituals often reflect the talents and interests of individual participants; they may respond to current events, the mood of the moment, the particularities of members' lives, or shared backgrounds and concerns. They may be playful, serious, mournful, silly, exploratory, or solemn, depending on the perceived needs of the group. They have an ad hoc quality—successful attempts may be reiterated or revised, whereas failures are seldom repeated.

Handbooks and Texts

Handbooks and texts are rare. There is an inherent resistance against recording texts for women's ritualizing. This is partly because, as Mary

Collins notes, "liturgical theory has long asserted the primacy of the performative ritual word over symbolic ritual action"; but for women "performative embodiment of relations seems to take clear precedence over performative utterance as a way of expressing religious meaning."[56] Women's communities have generally stressed the provisional quality of the textual artifacts of ritual planning.

ritualizing **emerging patterns in women's ritualizing**

emerging patterns in women's ritualizing emerging patterns in women's ritualizing emerging patterns in women's ritualizing

Women's rituals evidence considerable similarity across societies and theological types, even allowing for individual and cultural differences. This suggests that there may indeed be something we can call women's ritualizing (particularly in the contemporary West), with elements that are, if not unique, then commonly stressed when women worship together. Notwithstanding wide divergence in the way elements are combined and in the particularities affecting different worshipers, it is possible to construct a list of ritual elements that frequently appear when women ritualize. Although these items are neither singular to women nor exhaustive of women's practices, taken as a whole, the list offers an overview of what women's ritualizing looks and feels like in practice.

Lists of common elements in women's worship are not new. Several theorists have undertaken the difficult task of trying to define the ritual patterns emerging in women's spirituality communities. Most of these have focused, however, on outlining general principles or qualities of specifically feminist ritualizing.[1] They also tend to discuss theologically contextualized women's spirituality in, say, Jewish, Christian, post-Christian, or pagan traditions. Moreover, although feminist theoretical and ethical grounding is a crucial task, it does not address directly the evidence of ritual activity, nor does it encompass the wider scope of women's spirituality, which includes groups that may not be prepared to fully embrace extended feminist philosophy.

Because, as David Kertzer has commented, "we are what we do, not what we think,"[2] attendance to ritual behavior—not just ritual intentions or ritual principles—is appropriate and necessary. What do women actually *do* when they assemble to worship, regardless of whether they are led to do these things by culture, myth, planning, ideology, or inspiration? Liturgiologist Paul Bradshaw has observed that scholars of religious ritual generally engage in one of two strategies: "scattering" or "gathering." The task at hand here is one of gathering—defining, outlining, and typing the varieties of women's ritualizing in an attempt to identify commonalities and to provide an overview of a newly emerging field.

The evolving features of women's ritual action can be grouped, for convenience, into three categories: ritual images (recurrent metaphors and symbols), ritual elements (specific ritual behaviors or actions), and ritual characteristics (foundational presuppositions of women's ritualizing activity.) Taken together, these frequently observed elements provide a fair indicator of actual practice in women's groups and an outline of coalescing patterns.

Ritual Images

The Circle[1]

Few images encapsulate the spirit of women's ritualizing as effectively as the circle, and few women's rituals are conducted in any other arrangement. Casting a circle—an ancient practice recovered by women of many spiritualities—"creates a safe space, a space for women to be who they are."[3] Such a configuration also makes it possible for ritual participants to most fully interact with one another: "Choose a spiral dance or circle dance so people can embrace and sway," suggests liturgist Dianne Neu.[4] American Buddhist Michelle Levey notes that meditation in a circle "with just women together is a real treat."[5]

Beyond these practical considerations, the circle assumes a variety of deeply rooted metaphorical associations: the womb, the embrace, the spiral dance, the moon, the earth, the mandala, the bowl, the font. The St. Hilda Community, as one example, understands the circle to be a symbol of "containment" that "includes and births the divine in us."[6] In 1988, several hundred women from the European Forum of Ecumenical Christian Women joined in a circle dance in the well at the Anglican cathedral in Liverpool, "as a way of claiming their space but also as an illustration of our unity and sisterhood."[7]

The circle is also the dominant image in the dimension of time. Women's rituals tend to emphasize the cyclical rather than the linear: the recurrence of menstrual periods, seasons, moon phases, harvests—the endless cycle of life.[8] This perspective stands in contradistinction to the linear temporal images of the Bible and their oppositional pairing with metaphors of changeless eternity.

Horizontality

The extension of circularity is horizontality, through which women's ritualizing is liberated from the excessive verticality typical of male-focused religion.[9] Women's ritual actions tend to be grounded, nonhierarchical, spreading, and community centered. Eschewing metaphors suggesting rank, dominance, and ascendancy, such as the need to "climb Jacob's ladder" to reach a god "up in heaven" to whom they "lift up" their eyes, arms, or voices, they generally adopt instead tropes that suggest the equivalence of persons and the immanence of divinity within the horizontal earthly plane. For ritualizing women, sacred space is defined by the places where they work, love, parent, gather, birth, dream, relate, remember—places circumscribed by the horizon.

Nature

Women are reclaiming the association with nature that in earlier centuries, especially in the West, was the mark of woman's dishonor. Not only are ritualizing women embracing this ancient connection, but they also reject the automatic equation of nature with incivility, animalism, or shameful sexuality. At the same time, women are increasingly owning the earthy, fecund, sensual aspects of their nature and reinvestigating the ancient imagery of their relatedness to growing things, to fertility, and to the earth (or moon).

In women's worship, this is reflected in, among other things, a keen environmental sensitivity, a deepened appreciation of women's fruitfulness, and, for some, the practice of natural magic. In a more focused way, the movement toward Gaia theology—an earth-centered spirituality that perceives divinity in the living earth (with or without representing the planet as "Mother Earth" or as a goddess)—embodies this return to an appreciation of the power and ultimacy of nature.

This perspective is not without its critics, however. Catherine Roach, for example, urges a rejection of the equation of earth with mother. Not only might it be ecologically irresponsible to consider the earth, as we have our mothers, the provider of all wants, the disposer of all wastes, and the endlessly responsive nurturer, but also, she notes, the metaphor of earth as mother is undesirable because of the problematic associations with both of these terms in patriarchal culture.[10]

The Body

Related to the prominence of nature as a ritual image is an emphasis on the body as a vital, inexhaustible, and beautiful symbolic source. Recognizing that "the body is our first and last outward reality" and that "it defines and conditions our life experience,"[11] women generally celebrate themselves as embodied souls. In addition, women's ritualizing assumes that the body is a primary source for ritual metaphors and that sensory experience, in all its variety, constitutes the principal channel of revelation and sacredness. As Marjorie Procter-Smith notes, "Memories and experiences of the female body and its rhythms are no longer either marginal or negative, but central to a more complete understanding of God, self, and community."[12]

Furthermore, women's bodies are not understood to be ritually, naturally, or biblically impure or dangerous. Consequently, women's purificatory rituals, infrequent as they are, tend to focus not on the body but on the pollutants accrued from the compromises and depredations attendant upon living in society. Defilements and trespasses of women's bodies are also ritualized in contemporary groups; Ruether's *Women-Church*, for example, contains suggested rituals for healings from battering, rape, incest, abortion, and miscarriage.

Finally, the cycles and rhythms of women's natural reproductive and aging processes are, more and more, being ritually honored. Ruether includes liturgies for menarche, menstruation, menopause, and croning (a ritual recognition of a woman's status as a source of elder wisdom). Such rituals are increasingly common in women's liturgies.

Childbearing and Mothering

When Ruether first outlined some ritual suggestions for Women-church, she included several examples of rituals focused on childbirth.[13] The uniqueness and intensity of women's reproductive role make it a particularly evocative metaphor for women's spirituality and a deep resource for ritual action. For Sered, motherhood is one of the prime experiences addressed by women's religions, "a fundamental image, a key ritual focus, and a chief theological concern."[14] Indeed, so crucial is this image to women's ritualizing that a collection of services for women in the Reformed tradition has been titled *Birthings and Blessings*.[15]

More recently, however, some women's groups have expressed reservations about overemphasizing reproductive imagery, recognizing that childbearing is not part of the experience of many women—nuns, other celibates, the childless, and most lesbians, for example—and that stressing the role of women as childbearers reinforces patriarchal attitudes. Sered suggests that the physiology of childbirth is generally overlooked in the religions she documents (though it clearly is not in feminist spirituality); she sees the emphasis laid more strongly on its social implications—the relationship with a new person, the expectation of nurturing, and so on.[16] These objections notwithstanding, imagery rooted in fertility, pregnancy, birthing, nursing, and parenting remain central to women's ritualizing—and often difficult for others, as the brouhaha over the worship service at the 1993 Re-Imagining Conference has shown.

The Ordinary

Just as familiarity and comfort with their bodies inspire women ritually, so do the rhythms and activities of everyday life. In this vein, Caron suggests that "the first function of religious rituals is to connect the ordinary experiences of women's lives."[17] This emphasis on the ordinary has two distinct but related aspects. First, it celebrates the worldly rather than the transcendent. For example, Sered points out that, in contrast to the disengagement of the prevailing Buddhism in Burma, nat women are "absolutely involved in this world—with this-worldly passions, this-worldly desires, and this-worldly relationships." She goes on to describe how women's attention to relieving suffering in the here and now leads them "to sacralize profane experience, to enhance the quality of their current lives, to comprehend the supernatural already present within the natural world, and to invite the divine into their lives and even into their bodies."[18] Women's religions of more recent origin also incorporate this mundane approach, using metaphors and objects derived from everyday activities to characterize both the object of worship and themselves as worshipers.

The second aspect of women's embrace of the ordinary in worship is evident in the predominance of images of domesticity. As Sered comments, even for the most traditional of women,

> the holy may be totally embedded in the everyday world. The women described in this paper [elderly Jewish women in Jerusalem] inhabit a hallowed universe. . . . The basic building blocks of their religious world include shopping, sorting, cooking, serving, and cleaning.[19]

Cooking, cleaning, parenting, bathing, dressing, managing, sewing, networking, creating, teaching—the endless host of women's unglorified daily activities are being mined by women seeking a distinctive spiritual expression. Conversely, women have recognized the inherent ritualizing in the performance of everyday tasks.

Again, the connection between domesticity and ritual is not solely a contemporary phenomenon; Colleen McDannell notes that, in the nineteenth-century American home, "women, in the very pursuit of proper child rearing and housekeeping, engaged in domestic rituals."[20] That this focus on the home is not limited to North America is demonstrated by Susan Wadley, who says of Hindu women's ritualizing that "women's desires, as expressed in their rituals, are those of their world—the household."[21] This embrace of the environment, equipment, and ethos of domesticity is characteristic of women's ritualizing virtually everywhere.

Women's Crafts

An extension of the symbolic importance of everyday acts is the appropriation of women's handicrafts—what Procter-Smith calls "the woman-made world"—as ritual metaphors. Such images as weaving and quilting have come to represent, for religious women, the complex relationships and interconnections that pattern women's lives and spirituality. Barbara Walker, for example, suggests a ritual in which women "weave sisterhood" with yarn or dance.[22] Neu tells a parable to describe women ritualizing: "A woman revisioning ritual is like a woman who decides to make a quilt," it begins.[23]

The symbolic value of crafts predominantly produced by women comprises more, however, than a simple reference to the ways women spend their time. Handicrafts, especially domestic products, also have typically been devalued in patriarchal societies and a technological world. Their use in women's ritualizing thus sacralizes women's creative efforts, making the homely holy and reasserting the worth of women's work.

Procter-Smith makes the point that using symbols or objects from women's domestic work "serves to valorize work that is routinely devalued and exploited in patriarchal culture and religion." But she also issues a caveat: Ritualizing women must be careful to avoid instrumentalizing women's work and thus themselves becoming exploiters of the labor of women.[24]

Community

The image of community is a powerful one for women, particularly in feminist circles. Caron insists that feminist liturgy "is collective. It is created in communities committed to the well-being of women."[25] For many women's groups, ritualizing springs forth from the life of an existing community; in others, it is the creative and sustaining force that calls the community into being. For example, discussing the zar cult of North Africa, Sered comments on the role of community when a woman is "married to" a spirit: "Neighbors will not leave the afflicted woman alone. They sing, dance, and drum in front of her, promising to bring her whatever she desires."[26] In this case, an immediate community forms from the more general neighborhood in response to the ritual occasion. The same can be said of the spirit mediums of black South Africa; Susan Middleton-Keirn writes that "within this convivial sisterhood is a communion of equal individuals, who outside the group are inferior and marginal."[27]

The theme of community as the essence—indeed, as an organizing principle—of women's ritualizing is echoed in feminist liturgy as well. Mary Collins asserts that such worship "is effected not through elites but through the communal interaction of all the members of intentional groups."[28] Pagan traditions, too, as witch Starhawk comments, "are rooted in community. They are not religions of individual salvation, but of communal celebration and collective change."[29] Clearly, at the core of women's ritualizing, feminist or not, is a strong sense that women are not fully accepted members of existing communities and that worshiping in their own way is a powerful generator of new forms of community.

This urge to form meaningful groups has not been observed by all researchers. McDannell, speaking of religion in the lives of Victorian women in the United States, notes that "a strong notion of the group or the community is lacking. . . . Formal group worship takes a backseat to private devotion and informal moral influence."[30] However, the neat division of gender roles into public and private spheres, which she documents throughout her book, probably accounts for this seemingly anomalous pattern; moreover, women seldom had the opportunity to worship solely with other women. Further, it was precisely this milieu that gave rise to the powerful drive toward solidarity that was expressed in the suffragist and early feminist movements.

It seems more than safe to say that the community-building aspects of women's worship are near-universal. Once again, however, the stress on community must be balanced against a recognition of diversity, difference, and individual experience—an awkward tension.

Memory

Maria Harris has noted that memory, which she defines as "the telling, repeating, and recording of 'our' stories,"[31] puts people in touch with their communal history and allows them to integrate it into their worship in the present. This kind of remembering makes present those who have gone before and allows women to draw on their experience, wisdom, and power.

This image of the past reenlivened through the process of active memory is common in women's ritualizing. For example, at the core of the Christian feminist reclamation of the biblical tradition, as Elisabeth Schüssler Fiorenza has clarified, is an interpretive enterprise that features four hermeneutical principles: suspicion, proclamation, remembrance, and creative actualization.[32] This approach emphasizes "the common historical experience of women as collaborating or struggling participants in patriarchal culture and biblical history"[33] and the need to reclaim and own that experience. This process leads to a "subversive memory" that keeps alive both the sufferings and the hopes of women in the past while leading to solidarity in the present.[34]

The same principle is also operative in older, nonfeminist women's religions. For example, African American clergywomen in the Spiritualist churches of New Orleans frequently recount events in the life of their founder, Mother Leafy Anderson, not only to remember her contributions but also to validate themselves as ordained leaders who follow in her footsteps.[35] There seems to be a common understanding that women must remember their own heroes, leaders, and prophets or they will be forgotten by history, and that this process must be ritualized. In Mama Lola's Brooklyn Vodou community, "the people possess a memory more complete than that of any individual. Consultative ritualizing . . . helps the community guard against forgetting."[36]

Insight

If actively remembering those who have gone before is central to women's spirituality, its concomitant is a "concern for the subjective, intuitive feeling (instead of simply objective-rational thinking)."[37] Ritualizing women are liberated and guided by the imaginative possibilities of inner wisdom, creative memory, and emotional responsiveness, characteristics typically attributed to women but discouraged in conventional liturgical observance. In this context, qualities frequently portrayed as feminine in patronizing or mocking terms—"lady luck," "women's intuition," "old wives' tales"—are recovered as essential features of women's collective worship.

Thus, a contemporary ceremony will frequently incorporate poetry, music, or dance created by one or more of the congregants; a time of sharing personal stories and/or counseling; elements geared to elicit an emotional response; improvisational contributions; unstructured meditational or interpersonal time; or other opportunities to celebrate women's insight and creativeness.

The Shaman

The ritual image of the shaman—that is, of the skilled religious practitioner as healer, prophet, voyager, seer—has been preserved and honored in women's religions. Indeed, especially in the United States, many religions were founded by women functioning in just that role: the Shakers' Ann Lee, Theosophy's Helena Blavatsky, Christian Science's Mary Baker Eddy, Unity's Myrtle Fillmore, Spiritualism's Fox sisters, and so on—all of whom had charismatic, even eccentric personalities fueled by one or another kind of divine inspiration or vision.[38]

Non-Western women's ritualizing is frequently characterized by direct shamanistic activity (for example, in Korea or Africa), but even in the West, where religious leaders are not generally understood to be shamans, prophetic and visionary ritualizing is honored among women. Consequently, metaphors from shamanistic practices influence newer forms of women's ritualizing. Barbara Walker, for example, suggests women's ritual activities with names such as "the dark journey," "a guided meditation on the greater secrets," and "a ceremony of masks"—all using shamanistic images, metaphors, and trappings to achieve their effectiveness.[39]

Modern witches, too, recognize the ecstatic character of shamanistic worship. Indeed, Starhawk says bluntly that "witchcraft is a shamanistic religion." If not all Wiccans would make such a direct identification, most would acknowledge the importance of the ritual qualities that the image evokes. The ecstatic experience, continues Starhawk, "is the source of union, healing, creative inspiration, and communion with the divine."[40]

These images, of course, run counter to the priestly imagery that characterizes the familiar Christianity and Judaism of Western culture. Nonetheless, in their appeal to the inner, visionary world, to the power of imagination, and to the possibility of spiritual healing, they fit comfortably in women's ritualizing.

The Teacher

Members of Western religions are familiar with the image of woman as teacher, if for no other reason than the predominance of women as church school teachers. As McDannell notes, this image is deeply rooted in the social milieu of Victorian America, where "mother as teacher replaced father as priest and therefore as director of religious rituals."[41] In that setting, the Christian education of children became the paramount concern, and the mother was the key figure in that enterprise. As time went on, this female-identified activity was transferred to the church schools that accompanied or took the place of regular Sunday worship.

This modern conception of woman as religious teacher is also consonant, however, with views taken in more traditional cultures. One of the primary functions of the Sande secret societies of West Africa, for instance, is the passing down of wisdom and lore from one generation to the next. This is enacted both ritually (during initiation rites, the older women "make a show of instructing" the new initiates; in the ritual for childbearing, cult members stay up all night, dancing and teaching the dances to the young)[42] and pragmatically (while young women are segregated in the bush, they learn the myths, songs, and moral precepts of their people, as well as practical skills, from their elders).

In contemporary women's ritualizing, mutual instruction supplants command as the dominant mode of communication among worshipers. Older women are honored as sources of wisdom and connectedness; younger women are expected to bring freshness, new ideas, and vibrance to the group. Readings are frequently chosen from a variety of sources for didactic as well as aesthetic purposes and are generally reflected upon by the group as part of the service.

Empowerment

As Catherine Bell has demonstrated, ritualization is the deployment of strategies to construct power relationships and social reality. Virtually all women's spirituality groups—from contemporary North American feminists to Afro-Brazilian mediums to Northern Thai matrilineal cults—seek, through their ritualizing, to empower women or to help them feel less powerless.

Many of the women in these communities have experienced not only a lack of personal power but also the abuse of institutional power, both in society and in traditional religious settings. In response, ritualizing women metaphorically draw power from the moon, the goddess, the community, or other sources. Occasional rituals, such as Dianne Neu's "Celebrating Women's Power," address the issue head-on: "We need to affirm women's power, acknowledge its roots and use it to transform society."[43]

Ritual Actions

Reflexivity

Of all the elements common to women's ritualizing, perhaps the most distinctive and, especially in feminist groups, the most pervasive is reflection on the ritual as part of the ritual process itself. In describing the first women-designed service in a modern Jewish urban prayer community, for example, Riv-Ellen Prell-Foldes notes one major departure from traditional practice: "A discussion of the service was substituted for a Torah discussion, and a second postmortem discussion of the service, led by various women, followed."[44] Similarly, this technique was adopted by a group of Roman Catholic nuns celebrating the jubilee (fiftieth anniversary of profession) of one of their number; the ritual included an analysis of participants' reactions to various segments of the ritual. In doing this, they were following the experience some had had with the New York Women's Liturgy Group, which successfully incorporated reflexivity into its rituals.[45]

The community's dissection of the very act in which it is simultaneously engaged appears frequently in contemporary women's ritualizing. Sue Seid-Martin suggests this may be a gender-specific ritual element: "The research around gender communication styles shows that women are like that about their experiences and ideas; we like to set them out on the table. There they can be looked at, turned over and examined, contemplated, recast, mixed together, or discarded."[46]

Although he warns against allowing reflexivity to become a value in itself, Grimes nonetheless stresses its importance, especially for emerging ritualization, as "cultural self-consciousness" and the means by which a society constructs and critiques itself.[47] For women's spirituality groups, reflexivity internalized in the ritual is part of an egalitarian approach to the process of ritual creation and an acknowledgment that the process supersedes the product.

Naming

Heather Murray Elkins tells a story of a pastors' retreat at which participants were asked to share their spiritual name, the name they had given themselves. One young man answered, after a long silence, with the name his father had bestowed on him: "Not good enough." A spontaneous laying on of hands evolved in answer to the young man's pain—a ritualized, liberating response to a ritualized, oppressive naming.[48]

So potent is the act of naming that naming abusive or repressive events, persons, or attitudes in order to control or banish them is rooted in practice predating Genesis. One outline of ideas for feminist rituals lists, among a variety of suggestions for ritual naming, naming the circle ("opportunities for people to share their names in an interesting way"); naming participants' female family lines; naming friends; naming biblical women, liberating leaders, and loved ones; and naming "what we need to be healed from."[49] The first extended ritual act of the Re-Imagining Conference was a naming, in which various names for God were offered, along with various names of women and the names of the participants; and the theme of naming reappeared continually throughout the conference.

Naming ceremonies take many forms. The giving of a sacred name is an ancient ritual element, now often used in women's spirituality. For example, Ruether suggests giving a newborn child a name that is to be kept secret until puberty, or using naming as the high point in a women's ritual of initiation.[50] It may well be true that "the method of evolving spiritual consciousness of women is nothing less than the reclaiming of the right to name."[51]

Healing

"The most conspicuous similarities among women's religions emerge in the realm of suffering and healing," Sered says bluntly.[52] The age-old expertise of women as healers, midwives, nurses, and herbalists is claimed or reclaimed in many women's rituals. Indeed, women participate in healing rituals "nearly everywhere"[53] and are "bringing back ancient healing practices and inventing new ones that respect the power of the life energy."[54] Such ritual practices have never been lost in older women's religions. Whether African, Asian, or Western, these ritualizing groups attribute illness not only to the effect of germs but also to the action of spirit ancestors, to the damage done by violating taboos, to spiritual dysfunction, or to antisocial behavior.

Women's healing rituals easily cross the boundaries between pagan, Jewish, Christian, and Asian women's groups. Neu remarks that Christian feminists are deliberately designing "healing liturgies that support women surviving rape, incest, domestic violence, hysterectomies, AIDS, mastectomies, addictions, grief over choices they must make."[55] Yvonne Rand, a Buddhist, has developed a ritual for an abortion, a ceremony that provides "a means for people to be with what is so, no matter how painful that may be."[56] And Sered notes, citing Rodney Stark and William Bainbridge, that U.S. women are disproportionately represented in health and therapy cults.[57] For Wiccan women, healing is one of the principal uses of magic. Diane Stein considers it such a critical element of goddess spirituality that she specifies that all rituals must "contain elements of healing, change or transformation."[58] Walker suggests particular healing ritual activities of soothing and comforting, such as cradling, rocking, laying on of hands, and massage.[59]

Smudging

Smudging—a personalized use of incense—is another ritual element equally at home in a variety of women's spiritual communities. In contrast to the traditional Western use of incense—inherited from imperial times—in which it was burned and swung in a thurible to honor the powerful (king, deity, priest), ritualizing women use odiferous smoke as a sign of purification and a demarcation of ritual safe space. Stein discusses smudging in witchcraft, emphasizing that women use "the smoke and the process to let go of outside concerns and worries, to enter fully into the ritual."[60] The incense also appeals to and utilizes the olfactory sense, increasing the sensory stimulation of the ritual.

Frequently, rather than using prepared incense, ritualizing women circulate a bowl or bundle of smoking herbs—sage, for example. Each participant typically passes the herbs around her body or the body of other participants, wafts the smoke toward her nostrils, or perhaps directs the smoke to a painful or wounded part of her body.

Dancing

The rediscovery of liturgical dance within Christianity and Judaism, usually at the instigation of women, reflects the emphasis on movement that is natural to women's ritualizing. For the St. Hilda Community, dance "provides another mode of incorporating our spirituality . . . to express bodily the joy and pain" of life. One member of the group—the first to introduce dancing to the group's worship—comments that "it is so good to use our bodies, to bring our whole person to God, and to deepen the mood of a liturgy."[61]

Forms of expressive bodily movement such as circle dances, individual free-form dance, and narrative enactment are common in most women's ritual settings. Dances may often be quite simple, as in Afro-Caribbean dancing to invite possession by the loa or the orisha. In New Orleans Spiritual churches, affected in part by their African inheritance, as the Rev. Inez Adams, a bishop, says, "We dance. I've been to many Sanctified churches. They dance."[62]

Dance has the advantage of being sensual as well as symbolically expressive. Often, dancing is accompanied by the simple music of drum, flute, tambourine, or recorder.

Chanting

Chanting is another musical form common to women's ritualizing. Chants are easy to maintain without extensive instrumental support, promote solidarity and a sense of community, have a powerful austerity that enhances spirituality, and can be performed with little training or practice. Although "music plays a central part in feminist prayer" in North America, according to Procter-Smith, "feminist liturgy groups show a preference for communal song over solo, chant over elaborate polyphony."[63] Such choices have the advantage of simplicity, promoting the ability of all to participate. Seldom (if ever) is music in such settings elaborate, played to a silent audience, or performed by paid musicians.

Chanting is also the preferred musical form on the other side of the world, in Okinawan women's rituals, for example.[64] The singing accompanying Afro-Caribbean possession rituals is also extended chanting. Some songs, such as "She Changes," widely used in goddess rituals, take on the qualities of chant as the refrain is repeated many times. The extended responsive litanies typical of Dianne Neu's Women-church liturgies also assume the nature of chants as they progress.

Narrative

In the Western religious traditions, narrative is derived primarily from the liturgical use of scripture to recite the corporate myth. Women's worship, on the other hand, has no fixed textual tradition and no established mythical system. This is due, in part, to the omission of women's stories and contributions from the larger body of history of the major religions, but it also reflects a different approach to storytelling that characterizes women's liturgies.

For one thing, women tend to construct their communal history orally. The stories told in women's gatherings are often informal recountings of the lives of grandmothers or other ancestors, personal anecdotes from everyday life, confessions or intercessions, or autobiographical accounts. In feminist worship, these personal narrative units are deliberately set into the service—contrasted, perhaps, with short excerpts from the poetry or prose of women writers—to particularize the event as well as to preserve memories that would otherwise soon be lost.

Again, this is not a strategy unique to contemporary feminists. For example, in the New Orleans Spiritual churches, a repeated ritual element is the recollection of stories from the life of Mother Anderson. This serves not only to teach and conserve crucial historical information but also to reaffirm the activity and influence of the movement's founder in the lives of her followers.[65] Female Korean shamans make extensive use of narrative, not only relating their own autobiographical experiences but also eliciting public confessions of grief and pain from worshipers.[66]

Reverencing Ancestors

Closely related to, and often underlying, the extended use of narrative is the almost universal emphasis on reverence for ancestors (leaders, saints, heroes). Whether the ancestors are literal forebears, spiritual leaders of the past, founders of the religion, or simply those who are dead, almost all women's religions (and many that are dominated by men) ritually honor them.

In the Ryukyu Islands, both priestesses and families work at keeping the ancestors happy, well informed, and benevolent. In the rituals of a contemporary African American lesbian spirituality group, the members call out the names of their ancestors in a "spontaneous litany."[67] In one feminist pagan ritual, women are asked to call out the names of those dead people whom they would like to have with them in the ceremony—personal ancestors, famous people, victims of disease or disaster.[68] The close ties felt by the New Orleans Spiritual community to their religious founder, who is still believed to be accessible as a spirit, has already been noted. In the Muslim communities where zar cults flourish, women are expected to perform the rituals for historically important personages (Fatima, Husayn) as well as those for more recent saints and ancestors.[69] And in healing rituals among the Luvale women's societies, ancestral spirits causing sickness are asked to leave; Anita Spring notes that in this matrilineal society, women gain power through their own female ancestors.[70]

Mourning rituals, too, fall into this category. Generally, women are the chief ritual mourners; in many societies, it is the official job of women to handle mourning, thus freeing the men for more productive activities. Not only do these rituals provide, as Sered notes, social support for the mourners, a symbolic explanation for death, a heightened sense of community among women, and a proper send-off for the deceased, but they also often provide communication with both the newly dead and other interested ancestors.[71] Generally, this communication is in the form of spirit possession of a shaman (in Korea) or a medium (in Africa, the Caribbean, and American Spiritualism).

Using Natural Objects and Settings

Sara Maitland describes an occasion on which, with no prior intention, she and several other women "talked about the sea":

> We ended up throwing beach pebbles into its embracing infinity, naming each throw with the sins we wanted drowned, cleansed and forgiven, and alternately our own power and love that we wanted to reunite with the sea. It was both religious ritual and play, but it was using nature as a symbol both of our unity with nature and our unity with each other.[72]

Pebbles, the sea, and also trees, sticks, fruit, water, herbs, flowers, nuts, and other natural materials are frequently used when women ritualize. Plants and soil also have a place in women's ritualizing: at the 1993 meeting of the North American Academy of Liturgy, members were asked to bring dirt from home as part of the liturgy sponsored by feminists in the group. Ruether suggests, among other things, using salt as a symbol of wisdom and the unpotting of a plant as an image of relocation.[73]

These practices do not remain uncritiqued, however. As Procter-Smith notes, referring to the work of Teal Willoughby, the use of natural symbols by women can sometimes mirror the objectification and domination of nature long modeled in patriarchal traditions. She also warns against exploitation of the earth's resources, even symbolically—for example, by using water that is dumped back into its source or into the ground as an instrument for achieving spiritual purity. This implies the need for a heightened spiritual sense of what it means to "dispose" of something impure or unclean.[74]

Using Domestic Objects and Skills

As women's crafts have taken on metaphorical power in women's ritualizing, so too have the homely objects and abilities that reflect female domestic expertise. Rituals of sewing, quilting, banner making, and so on take place in a spiritual context in many women's groups. In some women's religions—for example, Korean shamanism—ritualizing takes place within the home itself and incorporates all the mundane features of women's domestic life. Sered ties this homely focus to women's stress on the this-worldly and immanent aspects of their spirituality, saying that "the physical sites, implements, and goals of women's religions tend to be indistinguishable from daily life."[75]

Eating

One domestic skill in particular, cooking (and eating), has a long history of association with women's ritual roles. As Sered puts it, "Emphasis on food and food preparation is one of the clearest and most common themes in the ritual systems of women's religions."[76] Among traditional Jewish Kurdish women, ritual cooking is the prime strategy for "constructing a meaningful religious life."[77]

In women's spirituality, eating assumes a quite different set of meanings than in the sacrificial cults of Christianity and ancient Judaism, more closely resembling the homely evangelical Protestant agape meal than the stylized feeding of the eucharist. Sered theorizes that the sacrificial meal, served in small symbolic portions, is a patriarchal development focused on the need to ingest blood to forge blood kinship; women's food rituals, on the other hand, focus on social ties and the ritualization of domestic skill.[78]

Postceremonial feasting is a crucial element in Afro-Caribbean ritual, whether Cuban, Haitian, or Brazilian. Brooklyn's Mama Lola typically spends a considerable part of her time planning, acquiring, and serving generous meals to, for, and in honor of various loa.[79] Among the black Caribs, "the sharing of food and strong drink both with the living and (through offerings) with the dead is a central ritual act."[80] Likewise, the women of New Orleans Spiritual churches lay out sumptuous offerings on an altar during rites for various saints; this food is later distributed to the worshipers. But this is not only an African-influenced practice; the same pattern is evident in St. Joseph's rituals among Sicilian American women; Kay Turner and Suzanne Seriff see these offerings of food as symbolic displays of women's reproductive and spiritual power.[81] In

Okinawa, Burma, and Korea, delicacies are also placed at shrines or household altars, to be eaten later either by the priestesses (if offered at public shrines) or by the family (in the case of domestic offerings).[82]

Contemporary groups have devoted considerable attention to developing effective ways to build on the traditional association of meal preparation with women. The Re-Imagining Conference used traditional breads from different parts of the world; a recent gathering of women ritual scholars shared a rice milk and honey concoction fraught with both maternal and religious significance. Procter-Smith recounts the efforts of a seminary class to develop a meal ritual: it was particularly effective because of its incorporation of narrative tales of cooking adventures and meaningful shared eating experiences.[83]

Ritual Characteristics

Spontaneity and Informality

Religious ritual is customarily perceived as a relatively fixed, rigid, repetitive activity with features assumed to lend the rite dignity, symbolic depth, and efficacy. Women's ritualizing, however, consciously fosters spontaneity, making allowance for the unanticipated—the inbreaking of humor, the unrehearsed poignant personal story, the surprising request for healing, the sudden urge to translate music or words into movement. Many ritual elements encourage participants to express themselves, often with unexpected results. Ritual leaders—when there are any—may lead prayer or meditation extemporaneously, further promoting a sense that the actions at hand are part of a process, not a fixed canon.

If spontaneity is part of the "motivation" of women's ritualizing,[84] then its dominant tone is informality, understood not as a lack of seriousness but as a willingness to be flexible and a respect for circumstances that put women at ease. Writers on women's ritualizing sometimes refer to this as the element of freedom allowed by women in liturgy. This freedom allows worshipers to "be themselves" and to avoid assuming formal masks of piety, but it also bans liturgical anarchy and self-absorption. On the one hand, it enables innovation, relaxation, and attention to the needs of the participants and the demands of the hour; on the other, it leads to intentional awareness of liberation as a political concern.

The De-emphasis of Formal Leadership

It often appears that the privilege extended to informality and spontaneity proceed, unchecked, into the planning and leadership of women's rituals—but not necessarily without awkwardness. One

planning sequence describes precisely the indecisiveness and immo-
bility that can result:

> The months that followed the retreat in which the Women's Ser-
> vice was ostensibly being planned were filled with the breakup
> and formation of network after network of planners. Only one
> woman of the original planners stayed involved in the service
> through all of the groups. From September to March the service
> belonged to any woman who was interested.[85]

Nonetheless, women have found that the advantages of a
nonhierarchical and nondirective approach to ritualizing outweigh the
risks. Theresa Berger makes the point that in their ritualizing, women
are agents, designing and leading their own worship:

> The task of liturgical design and leadership for women's liturgies
> is almost always exercised jointly; only seldom does the leadership
> lie in the hands of a single participant. This joint leadership re-
> veals the "egalitarian" nature of feminist liturgy; it consciously seeks
> to avoid distinctly hierarchical styles of worship.[86]

This attempt to achieve equal agency is worked out through techniques
such as rotating liturgical leadership, collaborative planning, and the inclusive participation of all. In the British Isles, for example, "the pattern
of sharing leadership in worship has been an important feature. Members
of the groups in turn take responsibility for planning, facilitating, and
writing liturgies."[87] Although it may be difficult to achieve these goals in
practice, they nonetheless remain foundational assumptions.

To some extent, this characteristic may represent a point of divergence between feminist groups in the Jewish and Christian traditions
and those in pagan or Wiccan communities. Goddess groups and witches
frequently focus ritual leadership in the figure of a high priestess, shaman, or other skilled presider. Cynthia Eller observes that although leaders of feminist ritualizing quickly deny any special leadership role, this
is a point of ambiguity for pagans. Both Starhawk and Z. Budapest, she
notes, try to downplay their obvious leadership positions in religions
that have traditionally stressed the powers of the priest/ess and seem
somewhat ambivalent on this score.[88]

Not all observers agree with this conclusion. Turner claims more generally that study of women's rituals reveals "the prominence of one individual as instigator or leader of the ritual." Although she acknowledges
that many rituals are leaderless, she goes on to remark that "a number of

women in the feminist community have emerged as ritualists, the counterpart of the shaman in traditional societies."[89]

With time, however, it has become increasingly clear that, at least in the West, egalitarianism is the goal. Catherine Wessinger reinforces this conclusion by observing that the fact that women's spirituality is consistently referred to as a movement, rather than as an institution, is itself an indication of the extent to which contemporary women, especially feminists, have gone to avoid authoritarianism and clericalism.[90]

Enhanced Roles for Older Women

Although Western society in general tends to devalue the contributions of the aging, Eastern and Western women share a common respect for elder women's role in ritualizing. For example, among black Caribs in Belize, mourning rituals are usually organized by the eldest woman related to the deceased. Moreover, "other older women provide most of the equipment and labor and, in some cases, small contributions of provisions and money." At some rites, older women are the only people in attendance, and at others, they are the central participants, available to offer skills and labor if necessary.[91] Similarly, in northern Thai matrilineal cults, the senior woman of the household is in charge of all family rituals; she watches the seasonal and ritual calendars for the family and each member, announces when rites will be performed, and prepares ceremonial offerings.[92] In Sande secret societies, the older women have the crucial task of teaching the young initiates the ethics, rituals, and lore of the group.[93]

Sered argues that elderly women take such an active role in religious leadership because their postmenopausal, post–child rearing status allows them the time and the autonomy to study ritual matters and exercise the detailed care they often require.[94] Stein offers the same argument.[95] Other factors—their freedom from menstrual pollution, the general respect for the elderly in many cultures, their greater knowledge base and wisdom, the prominence of the oldest female in a household, and so on—undoubtedly play a role as well.

It is certainly no accident that throughout Christian civilization, it has almost always been independent older women who have been accused of witchcraft. Fear and avoidance of old women have usually developed as concomitant cultural attitudes. Contemporary women's ritualizing groups often reclaim the honored status of the old woman, adopting the formerly pejorative English term "crone" to designate special status, and creating ceremonies to mark a woman's passage into that new category. Wiccans understand the moon to bring new wisdom to a postmenopausal woman at her croning ceremony; Ruether recasts this rite in a suggested Women-church ritual that is designed to combat social disdain, loss of self-esteem, and loneliness in aging women, as well as to affirm the wisdom and guidance they can contribute.[96]

Ecumenicity

June Goudey writes that women's liturgies "model inclusivity in all respects";[97] conversely, they intend to honor diversity as well. This can be a tricky ideal, as it may conflict with the equally valued principle of building community and consensus. It may not always be possible for, say, European American women, *mujeristas*, and womanist ritualizers, in a conceptual framework that consciously highlights their distinctions, to find sufficient commonality of image, practice, and meaning to enable an ongoing communal spiritual experience. Nonetheless, contemporary women's ritualizing seeks to identify and lift up those experiences claimable by all women through mutual ritual empowerment.

The argument for inclusivity may be somewhat more tenuous in other women's religions, but this is largely because those liturgies take place in very culturally rooted and geographically specific contexts; seldom do they require a deliberate focus on the inclusion of multiple cultural perspectives. Still, such liturgies do model this factor insofar as they cross socioeconomic boundaries and value the participation of each woman. When transferred to a more pluralistic setting, they tend to become more expansive. Even a cursory reading of Mama Lola's story, for example, highlights the breadth of the community invited to her Brooklyn ceremonies, although the Haitian culture in which her religion is rooted historically has been largely bounded by secret societies that have definitely not been inclusive.

Nonreliance on Texts

In general, women's rituals have a temporal, ad hoc quality, deliberately cultivated. As Procter-Smith explains, "The value expressed in a reluctance to publish liturgies may be characterized as a commitment to *contextuality*."[98] Each rite is understood to be rooted in the particularities of the occasion it observes, the group that enacts it, and the process that creates it; not only is the ritualizing of a given place and time perceived as unavailable for repetition, but it also raises questions of appropriation and attribution.

Additional factors have worked to keep women's ritualizing provisional. For one thing, in keeping with the inherently spontaneous and intuitive nature of women's spirituality, ritual texts, once used, are often discarded or exist only as outlines. Moreover, the evolving nature of

women's spirituality and the deliberately experimental quality of its ritualizing do not lend themselves comfortably to permanence. Women's
ritualizing also favors performative act over written text. Finally, women
are understandably wary of the uncritical institutionalization that trans-
forms ritualizing into rites.

Despite these concerns, the documentation of women's ritualization
is increasing rapidly. Ruether's *Women-Church,* at the forefront of the
movement, consists largely of ritual texts. The centerfold of each monthly
edition of *WATERwheel* reprints a women-church liturgy for use by
women's groups. Women's ritual texts also appear frequently in periodi-
cals and anthologies and are circulated in meetings, classes, and churches.
Ritual manuals for women, such as Walker's *Women's Rituals* and Rosemary Catalano Mitchell and Gail Anderson Ricciuti's *Birthings and Blessings* are proliferating. Although some of the literature, such as Dianne
Neu and Mary Hunt's *Women-Church Sourcebook,* still aims to be suggestive rather than prescriptive, the trend appears to be toward repro-
ducing thematic ritual texts.[99]

Extending the Analysis

Because contemporary women's ritualizing is continually changing
and new information is regularly coming to light about established
women's worship, it might be expected that any list of common elements would also be in flux. As an illustration, consider two ritual
elements that demonstrate the ambiguity and mutability of any such
typography.

The first of these elements is masking. Masking is hardly a common element in women's ritualizing, yet its occurrence in several contexts suggests that its ritual possibilities for women might still be evolving.

Masks and masking rituals have generally been assumed by scholars
to be the province of men. Until recently, the dominant theory on the
subject posited that masks had been the terrifying instrument men used
to wrest control of their tribes from matriarchal influences and hand it
over to male secret societies. Henry Pernet refutes this position, arguing
that masks are clearly used for ritual purposes and evoke symbolic, not
political, responses.[100]

In any event, masking is not altogether absent among women. The
most obvious use of masks by ritualizing women is among the Sande,
the African women's secret societies formed in response to the men's.

There, masked figures represent female ancestors of participants, and "if a man molests a Sande girl or infringes Sande rules, a masked Sande member arrests him."[101] When a Sande woman dies, her colleagues provide a symbolic reenactment of the masking ceremony allowed only to men.[102]

This example from an older religion illuminates a central issue arising from masking practices: power. And empowerment is a women's issue. The wearer of a mask accomplishes two immediate effects: she disguises her own identity (not a likely goal for most women in ritualizing groups, whose identities have all too frequently been denied or withheld), and she assumes a new, additional identity. The new identity of the masked person is not simply a comic or imaginary one; in most ritual masking, the wearer *becomes* the spirit or supernatural figure represented, thus temporarily, at least, assuming a more powerful persona.[103] Expanding this concept to include makeup and dress, Kathryn Allen Rabuzzi notes that "what unites the enormous diversity of ritual dress is an underlying belief that the special dress relates somehow to special power or powers."[104]

Masking as power is a complex issue for contemporary and feminist women's ritualizing, which seeks to legitimate and affirm the power in the life and experiences of the real person, not the disguised one. Some might object on these grounds to the use of masks by ritualizing women. Others might object to to what may appear to be cultural appropriation, although masking is part of almost every culture in one form or another and is psychologically universal. Nonetheless, masking has begun to appear when women worship. Many Wiccans, for example, use ritual makeup to create a ceremonial mask of power—not surprising, considering that the English word "mask" derives from *masca*, the medieval ecclesiastical term for witch. (This use of makeup to create a new identity recalls, among other things, the heavy makeup and costuming of Korean shamans.) Additionally, some feminists might laud the use of masks as appropriating a symbol of male dominance, thus negating its power to oppress.

Barbara Walker casts masking in a different light in her book of women's rituals, emphasizing its possibilities for playfulness and self-discovery, as well as for illuminating identity issues.[105] This new psychological focus highlights the diverse interpretations women are bringing to multivalent ritual acts. Whether masking will become a frequently used element of women's ritualizing will only be revealed in time; however, its adaptability, geographically diverse history, and potential for powerful symbolism make it an interesting case study.

The second ritual issue involves life-cycle rituals, or rites of passage. The issue here is not so much the appropriation of a symbolic act as the incorporation of an entire type of ritual activity. The question arises when Sered's research leads her to postulate, in bold letters, that "rites of passage are relatively rare and unelaborated in women's religions."[106] Superficially, this thesis seems reasonable, and it can be supported by the observation that women more readily perceive and objectify time as cyclical or spiraling, rather than historical; rites of passage theoretically reflect the more linear temporal thought of male-dominated religions.

But exceptions and objections to Sered's contention are numerous. For one thing, Sered bases her conclusion on the premise that women's religions do not pay much attention to women's bodies, being more concerned with social ties than with biology. Although the importance of social ties in women's communities cannot be underrated (recall that relatedness is the most frequently cited essential quality in feminist worship), the embodied quality of women's ritualizing, as I have described, is equally prevalent. Grimes sees culture and body as dialectical opposites but, as such, tightly linked: taking one seriously "always leads to the other."[107] And Caroline Walker Bynum also conjoins the two when she says of the crucial constituents of ritual, "Women's symbols and myths tend to build from social and biological experiences; men's symbols and myths tend to invert them."[108] The preeminence of relatedness as a necessary quality of women's ritualizing does not, then, preclude a similar emphasis on embodiment.

Even among the religions Sered investigates, there is clear evidence of a fuller embracing of women's bodies than is found in patriarchal religions; for one thing, none of them incorporate the outright condemnation of women's sexuality that characterizes, for example, developed Christianity. More positively, Sande, to take one group, pays considerable attention to women's bodies and their functions, especially in its initiation rites, as do most African-derived religions (such as Afro-Caribbean religions or the New Orleans Spiritual churches)—and indeed any that concentrate ritually on spirit possession (say, zar cults or American Spiritualism).

Beyond the complex question of embodiment, however, it is demonstrable that ritualizing women do develop rites of passage, though their emphases may not always be those of male religions. One passage that almost all women's communities seem to ritually acknowledge is death, as Sered's own research demonstrates.[109] Sande and Afro-Caribbean religion have complex initiation rites that occur at puberty or at the adult profession of faith (often closely coincidental events). And feminist groups are actively and deliberately developing rituals for every sort of life passage: indeed, almost every collection of ritual ideas for women includes liturgies for childbirth, miscarriage, adoption, commitments of various kinds, professional changes, divorce, croning, and so on. The general lack of childbirth rituals in more traditional religions, cited by Sered as evidence that women do not focus on life-cycle rituals, may in fact be due more to the uncertainty surrounding the survival chances of newborns than to a lackadaisical attitude toward their arrival.

It would seem that rites of passage, as a paradigmatic ritual form, do permeate women's ritualizing, though they are perhaps emerging in newly constructed ways. Time will determine whether life-cycle rituals become a greater factor in women's worship and whether they will ever assume a distinctive quality there. Like masking, this essentially masculine form of religious expression may prove to be too fraught with male philosophical dispositions to work well for most women; on the other hand, it may be appropriated and adapted by women into a new configuration that provides gender-specific, meaningful ritual.

space and time **ritualizing space and time** *ritualizing space and time ritualizing space and time ritualizing space and time ritualizing space and time ritu*

Ritualizing occurs and participates—fundamentally, inescapably, absolutely—in space and time. Such a truism may at first seem almost tau-
tological, but all too often religious ritual pretends to a transcendence
that is assumed to supersede somehow these core dimensions. Indeed,
since the 1957 publication of Mircea Eliade's *The Sacred and the Profane*, it has been widely accepted that the critical function of ritual is to
move the believer out of spatiality and temporality into an alternative
sacred reality.[1] This presumption is manifestly operative, sometimes at
the cost of awkward theological calisthenics, in a number of the so-
called world religions, as well as in some that are less well known.

In contrast, the emerging patterns in women's ritualizing make clear
its rootedness in the here and now, the earthly world of passing time
that constitutes the principle framework for human experience and value.
This distinction stands out so clearly that it deserves more detailed examination.

Sacred Space: The Dominance of Verticality

Tom Driver offers a scene that echoes the premise of *The Sacred and the
Profane*, in which Eliade elaborated a definition of sacred space that
depended on "the consecrating power of height."

> The building was split from one end to the other by an axis down
> its middle, the long center aisle, which ran from the street en-
> trance at the back right through the middle of everything and up
> the steps into the choir and up more steps to the bishop's seat, in

which he sat, at the highest end of this longitudinal line, and at
the middle of anyone's view who looked from the lay into the
clerical zone of the church. He was lifted up, and this elevation
pointed to things higher still, for his miter was pointed, and behind and above him rose the vertical cross of Jesus; and the eye
traveled, as it almost always does in cathedrals, to tall columns
and arches and high windows and decorated ceilings where the
mind's eye takes over and gazes still further up to the infinity of
heaven.[2]

For Eliade, the sacred, in the form of a sort of invisible vertical shaft,
breaks into the profane, horizontal world of "religious man," creating
an *axis mundi* at the point of intersection—a holy place, a vital locus of
access to the transcendent. Human settlement, worship, and aspiration
all cluster at this mystical place where the power of deity deigns to lower
itself to the mundane precincts of earth.[3]

Religious symbols reflect the relationship of earthbound humanity
to a sky-dwelling *mysterium tremendum et fascinans*: heaps of stone give
way to heaven-scraping temples and the spires of Christian cathedrals.
Literary and mythic references speak of ladders and staircases. The tower
of Babel was built, though not quite high enough. Verticality suffuses
the religious rituals of *homo religiosus*.

Although Eliade's vision, not intended to be normative, has more
recently generated considerable criticism on a variety of grounds,[4] and
although Christian liturgical theology contends that Jesus Christ has
erased the distinctions of sacred and profane, Eliade's description of
vertically oriented cross-cultural worship patterns is validated, in modern as well as archaic cultures, by simple observation of Christian church
architecture. Neo-Gothic cathedrals are still under construction—New
York's Cathedral of St. John the Divine, for example—and even country congregations long to be able to afford steeples for their places of
worship. Inside, long narrow spaces and vaulted ceilings draw the eye
inevitably upward, where it focuses on magnificent stained glass, outsized
roods, or elaborate reredoses. Chancels are raised, often well beyond the
need for clear sight lines. The altar, the "station from which earth looks
up to heaven,"[5] is elevated, often in tiers, and heightened with long
tapers.

Certainly, in the wake of the liturgical movement, some liturgical
architects produced multipurpose churches, simpler structures, and
spaces that reflected the centrality of the worshiping community. In-

creased attention was paid not only to the structural design of the architectural shell but especially to the interior arrangement; often these new patterns—semicircular seating, celebration *versus populum*, and so on—spoke eloquently of the theological infelicity of imaging relationships with God solely on a vertical plane. Yet in recent years, the "marked return to the monumental, the neo-sacred, and the neo-symbolic,"[6] both in new liturgical architecture and in the retrograde adaptation of modern worship spaces by congregations eager to return to more conventional models,[7] indicates that vertical, transcendent imagery continues to reflect the primary liturgical understanding of Christian worshipers.

If verticality is the evident mood of liturgical building and interior space, then it is perhaps even more apparent in ritual movement and symbolization. Typically, long columns of ritual participants process along the center aisle, symbolically moving not only forward but also upward.[8] Immersion baptism sinks initiates below ground level to raise them up again. Worshipers "enter the church by mounting the steps, themselves a symbol of the spiritual ascent on which [they] are now embarking."[9] The celebrant's invocations of God are accompanied by a panoply of gestures that unmistakably imply that God is "up"—raised arms and hands, uplifted eyes, hands clasped pointing skyward, and so on. A recent gathering of liturgists ritualized the singing of the triumphant hymn "Earth and All Stars" by standing on the pews—closer to the stars and to the assumed dwelling place of their source.[10]

Both anthropological and theological explanations are available for this obsessively vertical symbolism, but certainly one major factor is the continued influence of hierarchical structures in Western religion. As medievalists have demonstrated, church organization, doctrine, and rituals have been suffused with vertical symbolic patterns meant to mirror divine order.[11] The patriarchal underpinnings of hierarchical systems have long been established. Kay Turner, for example, has remarked that sacred space "is created as sacred by men and in most societies women have little or no access to it. Women live in the profane world, the world that is incapable of being transformed or of transforming those who live in it."[12]

But a more detailed look at the implications of vertical and horizontal imagery (and thinking) on liturgical practice was absent from the literature until Ron Grimes's article "Liturgical Supinity, Liturgical Erectitude: On the Embodiment of Ritual Authority."[13] Although Grimes admittedly writes somewhat tongue in cheek, savoring the sexual implications of his characterization of the vertical-horizontal dichotomy, he nonetheless addresses a topic of significance: "that gender issues (as distinct from sexual issues) are more fully determinative of both liturgical practice and liturgical theology than most white male theologians readily recognize or openly admit."[14]

Grimes's particular concern is the way that ritual authority is transmitted and maintained. His discussion turns on analogues of bodily posture—of vertical, male erectitude and horizontal, female supinity—which reflect differing models of authority and liturgical theology. His clear limning of the features of each posture vividly characterizes the contrast between vertical and horizontal ritual actions and their gender associations. Liturgical erectitude, "typified by poise and verticality," is hearty and robust; it maintains "a proper relation to tradition" and judges itself "superior to culture." Liturgical supinity, on the other hand, recognizes that "liturgy is essentially as cultural as it is religious" and focuses on ritual generation and creativity; it has a grassroots quality that employs "the symbols our culture would prefer to bury or forget, recycling and transforming them into tools useful for liberation of a captive liturgy."[15] Grimes goes on to call for the voluntary assumption of a horizontal viewpoint by the (male) guardians of liturgical erectitude, in the hope that this new position might provoke increased awareness of the vitality and creative energy of ritual freed from upright ossification.

Women's Sacred Space

For Eliade and his followers, sacred space is understood as the transcendent interjection of the vertical into the horizontal—the product of a quintessentially male act by a male deity who thereby clearly delineates sacred territory and sets it apart from profane space. Recent Christian theology confirms this view; comments George Worgul, "In sacramental behavior, the human imagination projects a vertical dimension which identifies the sacred object (God) as being above, i.e., in a position of power and transcendence."[16] For Worgul, the corresponding horizontal dimension is merely the time line from past to present to future.

As we have seen, many ritualizing women have attempted to expand the definition of the sacred horizontally into areas previously considered profane—the home, nature, the workplace. Thus, for example,

> Women-church declares sacred many of the elements that patriarchal Christianity has defined as profane: the body, sexuality, the home, ordinariness. . . . Much of women's lived experi-

ence and source of meaning has been forced to exist outside the boundaries of the sacred. . . . Women-church places pivotal elements of women's lives at the center of a sacred space *defined by women*. . . . [It] reclaims the living world as profoundly sacred and meaningful.[17]

Even this assertion, however, is not without its critics. Some feminists, such as Victoria Lee Erickson, decry the distinction of sacred and profane altogether, understanding sacred space to be specifically that space from which women are traditionally excluded, space in which "inclusive community was displaced by the sacred." Erickson asks, "Why do we need this center? Center of what? Center for whom?" and argues for the demise of the sacred/profane dualism altogether.[18]

Both critiques attempt to overcome the positionality of sacred space, the pinpoint definition that restricts sacred space to an intersection, a building, a monument, a hierophantic spot. In doing so, they project a horizontal expansion of sacred space into the world, into nature, into everyday life that is characteristic of women's ritualizing. In this horizontal movement, women locate the sacred globally yet not diffusely; sacred space is wherever women work, love, gather, dream, remember, relate.

Mary Daly, writing in a rather different idiom, reiterates the theme that spiritual women are redefining space:

Moving in Wicked directions, we open doors to Other dimensions, Other spatial perceptions. By thus reversing the reversals of the righteous space controllers, we enter a different context. Here Spinsters Spin on our heels, facing the "four directions" from different angles.[19]

For women attuned to this definition, sacred space is named and experienced horizontally—toward the four directions of north, east, south, and west—not upward and downward.

Anthropological research confirms that such spatial distinctions are not purely theoretical or arbitrary. Edward T. Hall, for example, in discussing how humans appropriate space, notes that "men and women often inhabit quite different visual worlds," then goes on to say that "the patterning of perceptual worlds is a function not only of culture but of *relationship, activity*, and *emotion*."[20] This observation links the very elements that many women would cite as the primary determinants of sacred space.

Not all women, of course, share a horizontal perspective. Women in traditional cultures, for example, still clearly envision God as "up." Susan Starr Sered reports that Kurdish Israeli women, who have gone on *aliya*, or have "gone up" in relocating to Israel, "firmly believe that God is in his heaven, that his heaven is located somewhere above earth, and that when speaking to or about God it is most efficacious to either look or move the hands in an upward direction."[21] The preponderance of Western women who continue to find their traditional religious affiliations fulfilling still think and respond spiritually in predominantly vertical categories, reflecting what they have been taught since childhood.

Nonetheless, experimentation with new ritual forms is expanding, especially in women-centered spirituality groups. Within that universe, ritual space is an issue of importance. Eileen King notes,

> My consistent observation about feminists is that as soon as they enter a space in which they are going to meet, some members of the group will start rearranging the furniture. . . . In the activity of pulling chairs and shoving tables women are identifying what they need and how those needs can be met. Women do not assume that a space, just because it is available to them, is suitable.[22]

Mary Collins, studying how churchwomen assume liturgical authority in times of change, notes that responsibility for the arrangement of liturgical space has traditionally been the one area of ritual expertise permitted to women, who have long been sacristans, musicians, and altar guild members who "arranged the furniture, set out furnishings, organized processional movements, set out the books." Thus, she continues, when women had the chance to develop their own rituals, it was hardly surprising that "they began by dealing with the familiar. No longer acceptable relationships were reordered symbolically by choreographing new spatial arrangements and rearranging sanctuary furniture. Relational symbols were handled differently or not at all."[23]

Sacred space, far from being simply an adjunct liturgical consideration, is a core datum in women's ritual experience. Its design, arrangement, rearrangement, and ultimate use are central elements in women's self-definition through ritual.

Women's Horizontal Ritualizing

Many of the emerging patterns discussed in chapter 2 protest verticality and contribute to an extended sense of sacred space. For example, as we noted, most Christian, post-Christian, Jewish, and pagan women's ritual events begin with gathering in a circle. The circle can be cast through a specific invocation of the spirits of the four directions (as in Wiccan ritual), can be created by hand-holding or some other simple action, or may simply be the form in which participants arrange themselves. In contrast to the typical forward-facing rows of church seating (oriented symbolically upward toward the altar), the circle is a horizontal arrangement that makes sacred all the ground space it circumscribes: "When we enter the circle, it is said that we enter a 'world between the worlds,' a sacred, liminal space where it is possible to enter into communion with the divine, step into the mythic, and actually alter the fabric of reality."[24] It also works to abolish dualisms—up/down, in/out, sacred/ profane. Although the circle encloses, it is not meant to exclude; it can be expanded infinitely as more participants enlarge it, and it implies an ongoing outward radiation.

Even though the circle seems a somewhat obvious ritual arrangement, adapted, in part at least, in the restructuring of some Christian churches during the period of liturgical renewal, criticisms arise when it is introduced into traditional settings. The circle, in any form, has not gained general acceptance in Christian liturgies. One liturgist summarizes the objections:

> First, the assembly ordered in a circle is viewed as too inward-looking. . . . Secondly, the circle-as-metaphor, complete and "perfect" as it is, is viewed as likely to misguide the assembly as regards its own incompleteness. Thirdly, . . . [a] full circle would require some folks to be behind the presider and preacher."[25]

Another states flatly, "The audience and the speaker must meet face-to-face, not in a circle."[26] For ritualizing women, unfettered by such ex post facto concerns, gathering in circles has been natural, automatic, and ritually successful. Not only is the circle a pragmatic ritual arrangement, but its symbolism reflects the experience of women's spiritual communities.

Criticism of the use of the circle seems to center on the role and relationship of the assembly to the priest or preacher. Perhaps one of the most hierarchical of all religious symbols is the (high) priest, a person perceived as set apart for special mediation of the divine. Most women's rituals consciously subvert such hierarchical leadership roles in favor of an egalitarian and horizontal model of rotating, shared, or minimized leadership. Even when a woman is reading, leading a reflection, or otherwise exercising a ritual gift of leadership, she is unlikely to move from her place in the circle and rarely stands on a raised dais or assumes a position implying superiority or separateness. This is evident, for example, in the "rite of healing from distress of mind or body" found in Rosemary Radford Ruether's *Women-Church*.[27] In many ways, this ceremony echoes familiar Christian healing rites, but it replaces the priest as the traditional conduit of healing with a group of the sick woman's friends, who lay hands upon her in various places, lead her through a meditation on healing forces, and finally come together in a shared embrace.

Another element that lends itself to new spatial relationships is the emphasis in women's ritualizing on the ordinary events and experiences of women's lives. Take, for example, the figurative and literal quilt so eloquently discussed by Dianne Neu and so frequently a part of women's rituals.[28] The image of the quilt is not used accidentally by women. A quilt is homespun, created, flat, horizontal, spreading, secular, narrative. It draws in, includes, comforts, represents, and remembers.

The recognition of the holy character of domestic life extends to domestic space as well. Whether women participate in space generally regarded as sacred, make their own spaces sacred, or bypass the category of sanctified space in favor of an appreciation of their own precincts, they are in accord that sacred space is not located solely in consecrated buildings, or even on mountaintops. Worshiping women allow for the sacredness of mundane spaces—the kitchen, the laundry room, the children's bedroom—"where the breaking open of old expectations and visual patterns allows for the in-breaking of the Spirit. . . . Each space has its own feeling and unique possibilities for eliciting both reverence and interaction."[29] Sacredness in these spaces is a product not of the extraordinary presence of a deity or the performance of consecratory rituals, but of the women who inhabit the spaces and stamp them with their own indwelling holiness. Even in Islam, "'Every house has its own sacrality.' . . . The adage implies that not only does every house have a sacral character, but that this sacral character is dependent upon the presence of women."[30] Domestic objects and actions are peculiar, if not exclusive, to women's worship, and they convey a distinctive sense of the sacred that demolishes the sacred/profane dichotomy:

> If we take as women's rituals and women's symbols the rituals and symbols women actually use, and ask how these symbols mean, we may discover that women have all along had certain modes of symbolic discourse different from those of men. Even where men and women have used the same symbols and rituals, they may

have invested them with different meanings and different ways of meaning.[31]

Similarly, women's rituals are supinely earthbound, in close touch with nature. For some Wiccan and goddess groups, Gaia herself is the deity, the primordial earth mother, the source of strength, the ultimate destination; rituals for these groups, as the witch Starhawk describes, are always earth-centered: "The first element to plan carefully is grounding. For a ritual to be powerful, we must start grounded, stay grounded, and end grounded, because the power that we raise comes into our bodies through the earth, and then returns to the earth."[32] Only a rare women's ritual does not make some reference to this spatial relationship. Barbara Walker suggests, for example, that meetings be held, if possible, "in someone's yard, garden, woodlot, meadow, or field"[33]—in other words, in flat, wide-vista, horizontal outdoor spaces.

In their focus on the sacredness of earth, visible from horizon to horizon in a great planar circle, modern ritualizing women have stopped looking skyward for transcendence and have defined sacred space as area, not as point. Moreover, it is a space they inhabit comfortably, bodily. Women use embodied rituals that establish horizontal relationship (hugging, hand-holding, touching for healing) and that require sideways movement (dancing, swaying, changing postures). This is not accidental. Grimes, on the orientational distinctions of liturgical dance, comments that "when dancing shifts from circularity and symmetry to linearity and asymmetry, the religious climate is likely to shift from prophetic criticism to priestly conservatism."[34] The horizontal movement of women's ritual dancing helps maintain the pervasive mood of spontaneity, openness, social awareness, and flexibility that are characteristic of women's ritualizing.

Rituals by and for women's bodies have ancient roots; many are only now being made part of public ceremonies. Whatever their source, whether old or new, body rituals ground women in the world, in a space where creatures that walk, crawl, lie supine, squat, grow, ache, laugh, touch, moan, and regenerate are more sacred than those that float eternally insensate in the clouds.

The inherent horizontality of religious ritual experienced, developed, and reclaimed by women frees it from the bonds of verticality and allows it to spread out. And in spreading, it reaches beyond the small community where it originates, beyond the larger religious organization (if any) surrounding that community, beyond religious applications at all.[35] This expansion leads to a significant crossover between women's ritualization and the wider secular culture.[36] When women are ritualizing, religion and culture are perceived as cooperative, conjoined, inseparable, part of an integrated whole. Women are freer to perceive the holiness of living and of human relationship, and to incorporate them into a religious worldview. For feminists, this means integrating issues of politics and justice with ritual; for more traditional women, it may mean an increased need for inclusivity, a call to church leadership, a greater commitment to social outreach, or the introduction of rituals for occasions formerly considered properly in the secular realm, such as healing for rape or abuse, divorce rites, or adoption ceremonies. Women's ritualizing crosses over what patriarchal religions perceive as an inherent boundary between believers' "profane" behavior and their expected religious behavior.

Although this crossover effect has encouraged the incorporation of cultural and domestic artifacts and rituals into women's spirituality, it also extends outward, influencing other cultural and religious practices. For example, although Kwanzaa, the African American winter holiday, began in 1966 at the instigation of an African American man—Maulana Karenga—and has been largely organized and popularized by men, the rituals of Kwanzaa are hearth rituals—domestic, family-oriented, and clearly female in both origin and execution; as actually practiced, Kwanzaa, in style and content, is very much a women's ritual. Kwanzaa was originally conceived as a secular alternative to Christmas, but now it is understood as a complementary ritual, largely because many African American women were unwilling to abandon their Christian religion in favor of a purely cultural celebration. As Kwanzaa is now celebrated, it includes elements of both African tribal religion and Western Christianity, as well as African and American culture. In this case, women's influence has blurred the traditional religion/culture boundary. In general, women's ritualizing appears to expand outward from the narrower religious sphere into the larger context of culture, melding the two realms into a fairly agreeable alliance that has proven to be a comfortable medium for women's spirituality.

Horizontal Ritualizing: A Case Study

The horizontal elements of women's ritualizing just described can be easily identified in almost any typical women's liturgy. It may be illustrative to examine one in some detail. The following Women-church liturgy, chosen pretty much at random, is a brief thematic ceremony called "Celebrating Women's Power."[37]

The first action of the ritual, "preparation," suggests creating a circle of chairs, reiterating the emphasis on the circle as the most felicitous arrangement of women's ritual space. The gathered women then "name the circle" by "focusing women's power," looking into a kaleidoscope, naming themselves, and sharing their thoughts on issues of women's power. The next action, the "call to gather," echoes the theme of coming together in a circle. One of the readings, a poem, tells how a "rainbow serpent covers me, head to foot, in endless circles." The circle theme is also repeated in a dance that concludes the liturgy.

Leadership is established beforehand. Because this is a written liturgy, developed by an expert for use by others, it suggests, to some degree, a traditional model of ritual leadership. However, it advises that different people lead separate parts of the ritual and that they use their own words rather than only the text presented. Other than the readings, which require a single lector, all the ritual actions are either simultaneously or sequentially communal. No so-called high priest is present.

Homespun symbols are very much in evidence—a child's toy (the kaleidoscope), a cutout paper heart, a candle, a weaving. All are incorporated into the ritual and interpreted in terms of women's power over their own lives and in concert with others. The symbols are placed in the center of the circle as a point of focus during readings that reflect on issues of relatedness (heart), divinity (candle), and solidarity (weaving). Actions, too, are simple and down-to-earth—chanting, reflecting together conversationally, dancing without choreography, sharing nonsacramental (but nonetheless symbolic) food and drink.

Earth-centeredness is apparent in the use of a bowl of smoldering herbs representing wisdom and the expelling of unfriendly spirits. Another earth symbol (and circular image) used in this particular ritual is the egg, representing the self during the reading of a poem on self-awareness. The readings and songs themselves often refer to the earth: "Listen to the power within yourself / Calling out the messages of the earth and sea," and, "We're making connections from all earth's directions."

Likewise, this liturgy repeatedly adverts to characteristics of embodiment. To begin with, it incorporates the whole of sensory experience—looking through the kaleidoscope, smelling the burning herbs, listening to readings and singing songs, tasting food and drink, touching others. Gesture and movement accompany various aspects of the rite: arms, legs, bodies, and heads are used in a motion symbolizing the exorcism of abusive power; participants touch one another during a blessing for discovering their strength; embracing accompanies the exchange of a greeting. One litany exorcises attitudes of "believing women's bodies and souls are dirty, sinful and inferior." A reading says that "it is in touching one another that we become most fully ourselves."

The extension of this religious ritual into a wider cultural context is apparent in such elements as the deliberate use of a weaving from another country, accompanied by a reading stressing political action in attending to the environment, stopping global conflict, and legislating for humane goals. The whole issue of power, of course, around which this liturgy is constructed, is a presumably secular concern rooted here in religious ritual action. The religious and secular aspects of power— where it comes from, who has it, what it should be used for, and so on—are inextricably entwined in this rite, confirming Catherine Bell's observation that "ritualization always aligns one within a series of relationships linked to the ultimate sources of power."[38] Or, as Grimes puts it in his direct way, "Let us not pretend that this is not a power struggle."[39] For ritualizing women, no sharp delineation between religion and culture can be made, in this or in the multitude of other issues women understand to be properly addressed ritually.

Space and Power

Women's reevaluation and redefinition of sacred space is not merely a matter of taste or even style. Rather, it reflects a core concern that harks back to the power issues elucidated by Bell. "Women have discovered that *where* they worship, *where* they place their bodies in worship, is very significant," as Rees notes.[40] This significance derives not only from women's need to develop and use meaningful symbols that open up their ritualizing to depths of meaning and possibility, but also from the necessity of claiming their own territory. As Procter-Smith writes,

> Reorienting a space declares clearly and unambiguously the creation of a domain of power and control. . . . The need for power and control of space for prayer arises out of the knowledge of the suffering women have endured and continue to endure in traditional church spaces.[41]

Although many feminists have recently voiced concerns about women's assumption of the mantle of victimization, Procter-Smith's point, despite her vocabulary of suffering, is that spatial positioning can be determinative, both metaphorically and pragmatically, of the relative, real-world positions of the persons and classes involved. Like language, spatial symbology is so powerful as to create the reality it expresses.

This effectual power is evident, for example, in the preconciliar Roman Catholic rite of adult initiation, as Catherine Vincie has discussed. Noting that "language makes up only part of the symbolic vocabulary of all rituals; placement in space and order in time are two other symbols that function to inscribe gender," she remarks that in this ceremony, male baptismal candidates were instructed to stand on the right, whereas women were to stand to the left. Vincie notes,

> It is nearly impossible to read a gender neutral message into the text. In light of the general cultural preference for right over left, the biblical alignment of the right with goodness and the misogynist tendency of the tradition to connect women with evil, one can only conclude that such placement served the positive affirmation of men and underlined the secondary, if not negative, status of women.[42]

The gendering of space, then, is more than a simple issue of liturgical preference; it also relates to key themes of autonomy in worship, the reclamation of surrendered territory, and the ability to evoke the "holy" appropriately.

Such an observation implies that the concept of sacred space be taken literally as well as figuratively—that is, that ritualizing takes place in "real" space. Both Vincie and Grimes discuss this in relation to the work of Victor Turner. Grimes disputes the assumption of Eliade, Arnold van Gennep, and Turner that sacred space is largely metaphorical. Only recently, Grimes says, "under the impact of the environmental crisis, critiques by feminist theologians, and the emergence of ritual studies, sacred space is beginning to be taken with a new seriousness and conceptualized with a concreteness previously absent."[43] He goes on to make the case for consideration of sacred space as real space, not utopian or transcendent space, and for a recognition of the criticality of space to ritual activity and efficacy.

Vincie goes further, arguing in tandem with Bruce Lincoln that ritual evocations of space in initiation rites for men and boys differ from those for women and girls. The Turnerian descriptions of linear movement through space and through the phases of initiatory rites—from separation through liminality (transition or threshold) to reaggregation—do not apply equally. Indeed, Vincie claims, "the metaphor of location does not appear to be helpful in describing women's rituals since initiation rites for women tend to have the initiands remain within the domestic sphere rather than changing location as is typical of men's rites."[44] Again, women are found inhabiting domestic space during ritual moments. In traditional initiation rites, however, this is space assigned by the dominant culture; it is unimportant space, a space for "putting a woman in her place." When women consciously place themselves in their homes and gardens for worship, however, these spaces assume an entirely different coloration. Thus, the powerful element in women's choice of domestic settings for worship is their deliberate reclamation and sanctification of locations that were previously devalued and minimized as sacred sites.

Conclusion

In his article on liturgical posture, Grimes fantasizes an anthropomorphized scene in which liturgy and culture assume personalities that conform to the normative expectations of traditional ritualizers who argue that liturgy should remain immune to the incursions of culture. In this scenario, "liturgy is vertical, male, and standing erect; liturgical authority walks tall. Culture, now obviously female, is supine and vulnerable. To be lying on one's back is dangerous, not to mention bad liturgical style. It is an invitation to abuse."[45]

Religious women, long accustomed to this position, are increasingly declining the invitation. Rather than confronting traditional liturgy, they are scuttling sideways, distancing themselves from its rigid upward imperatives. Rather than trying, as they have in the past, to jostle for standing room only in a vertical ritual universe, they have begun to use the insights gained from generations of being stretched out against the earth. Their experience of supinity has yielded a fertile ritual vocabulary that resonates with women's spirit and enlightens new paths to the sacred.

Sacred Time: The Dominance of Linearity

To live in today's world is to live on a time line. With the advent of historical consciousness, the concept of time quickly assumed a linear aspect that so dominates the modern perception of reality that it is virtually universal. Contemporary people find it very difficult to imagine time as anything other than a steady, inexorable march into a future of continued progress and evolution.

That such a view is essentially male is easy to argue. The same biological imagery that characterizes classically sacred space applies to time as well: time is forward-thrusting, a phallic arrow pointing ahead to ever greater control of the human environment, lifestyle, and society. Time is the portal to unexplored vistas of challenge, opportunity, adventure. Time is meant to be conquered, harnessed, efficiently managed.

Time is also finite. Mary O'Brien bemoans the "fixation with finitude" that she sees as distinctively masculine, "the preoccupation with death, the despair; the new romanticism which sees eternal return as the no-longer-courageous, now merely pointless cycle of the natural world; a mindless on-spinning continuum of triviality."[46] Linearity and finitude, in best Western style, dictate a life-model of birth, aging, and final demise—and, consequently, the religious imagery of heaven, hell, and eternal rewards, as well as datable events: the Eschaton, the Second Coming, the Last Judgment. Such images ultimately participate in a philosophy founded on conquest, achievement, legacy, triumph, dynasty, and lordship—a perspective that generally is more amenable to and reflective of the values and longings of men than of women. As Elizabeth Deeds Ermarth remarks, patriarchal conceptions of time can be damaging to women: "So long as time means what our novelistic and social conventions generally have told us it means, women's acceptance or incorporation as autonomous subjects in the discourse of history is simply impossible."[47]

Women's Sacred Time

Not surprisingly, the view of time incorporated into women's ritualizing rarely echoes the themes of linear temporality. Neither is it identical with Eliade's idea of sacred time, although the two perspectives have more in common in the discussion of time than of space. For Eliade, sacred time is mythic time—repeatable, representable, and renewable through ritual. Although he refers to sacred time at one point as "circular," his imagery more generally describes a kind of parallel universe of timelessness rather than a world in which "real" time is cyclical. Eliade's primitive religious tribes, clearly not linear and progressive in their time consciousness, regularly "return" to the time of eternity, in which reality remains unchanged. Among women commentators, Riv-Ellen Prell-Foldes would seem to agree, saying that "one task of ritual is to present events as timeless, to mask and limit change, to reiterate the past within the present."[48]

O'Brien, however, clearly distinguishes women's view of time from the Eliadean perspective, noting that "feminism is a clear example of the power of cyclicality, not a romantic eternal return but a never-going-away."[49] Moreover, many women would deny the desirability of defining ritual as timeless and changeless; change is, after all, another familiar characteristic of women's lives. ("Everything she touches changes" goes the well-known chant for the goddess.) Neither this model nor the modern paradigm of serialization seems to resonate strongly in women's ritualizing. Rather, the image that once again dominates for women is the circle—in this case, modified into a spiral, cycling forward (after all, women, too, are modern persons, acutely tuned to historicity), expanding, yet tied to the rhythms and seasons and loops of nature. The refinement of understanding the circle as a spiral is significant and is rooted in perceptions of reality. Even in a cosmologically ordered culture, with its preference for a masculine sky god, "time is nothing other than the movement of planets and stars in space . . . spiraling movement."[50]

Classically, as well as in today's manifestations of women's spirituality, women's connection with nature has led to a view of time that reflects, particularly, the association of women with the cycles of the moon. First, and most obviously, the menstrual cycle reproduces lunar and tidal cycles. Second, representations of the goddess, both ancient and contemporary, often make her a lunar deity,[51] frequently accompanied or figured by a snake—the animal that regularly sheds its skin in a continuing spiral of growth and new life. Women's bodies, perceptions, and daily lives are profoundly affected by this undulating rhythm of reproductive potential, confirming the infelicity of trying to conform their worship to a purely sequential, unrepeatable view of time.

The circle, then, is the dominant image not only in the dimension of space but also in the dimension of time; women's rituals tend to emphasize the cyclical—the recurrence of menstrual periods, seasons, moon phases, harvests; the endless cycle of life, death, regeneration. This perspective reiterates many of the common themes emerging in women's ritualization: the metaphor of the circle, the importance of nature, the centrality of body and reproductive imagery, and so on.

Nonetheless, this easy equation must be tempered with critical wariness. Frieda Johles Forman cautions against a facile identification of women with nature:

I do not regard [the feminization of time] as a return to lunar consciousness, nor a celebration of women's natural cycle. . . . As feminists, while not disowning our very real bond to the natural world, we must continue to resist the definition of women as nature: that is, we must live in the world as subjects whose transcendence is grounded in a generative temporality.[52]

Echoing Ermarth, Forman's concern is that women must not allow themselves to continue to be written out of history by refusing to accept their place in it or by opting out of it.

Women, Time, and Memory

In chapter 2, memory was identified as one of the images that permeate women's ritualizing. For women, the concept of memory is more than simply recollection, more than nostalgia; it is constitutive and substantive, remaking both past and future, subjectifying women's passage through time and history. As Forman says, "Memory is a labor of reappropriation, a remodeling of time."[53] Irma Garcia comments even more practically: "Woman uses her memory to break up the linearity of time."[54]

Women need time—even the sort of time that distinguishes past from present—for the invocation of memory and imagination. Garcia comments insightfully:

Women's mistrust of time translates itself into a return to time as lived day by day which is an affective time providing fertile ground for the awakening of memories, for moments, islets of silence, expectation, times-outside-time. All these moments which women refuse to forget encrust themselves in memory which plays an essential role in the life and literature of women.[55]

Both in literature and in ritualizing, the active engagement of memory frees the imagination of women to call forth a relationship of the human and the transcendent that takes place in the familiar and holy precincts of women's sacred space and time.

Living Archaic Time

Mary Daly has regularly gone beyond the accepted categories of space and time to redefine both what women understand those dimensions to be and what their import on women's lives and selves is. In her *Wickedary*, she defines time as what she calls "tidy time": "fathered time; measurements/divisions that cut women's Lifetimes/Lifelines into tidy tid-bits;

dismembered time, surgically sewn back together to mimic and replace Tidal Time."[56] This crafty summation reiterates Daly's earlier observations on the necessity of women reclaiming their own sense of time. Women, she asserted,

> are claiming/reclaiming our own Original Motion/E-Motion/ Movement. Refusing to join the archetypal act, we move into Time that is measured by Original Acts. Original Movements/Acts are by definition creative. Original Women, Spinning off limits . . . [enact] the elemental shedding of patriarchal time that is essential to the Movement into and creation of an Archaic Future. As women move more and more into Living Archaic Time, our Original, Creative Time, we Realize ourSelves.[57]

ritualizing narrative and women's ritualizing
narrative and women's ritualizing narrative and women's ritualizing narrative and women's ritualizing

Women tell stories—personal, poignant, preserving, prophetic—whether in Native American cultures, where women's ritual storytelling passes on folk wisdom and ethical norms; in Korea, where women shamans relate the messages of the ancestors to paying clients; in the Madhya Pradesh area of India, where women ritually gather to tell stories after the birth of a child; in Morocco, where Muslim women tell their stories for healing at the shrine of Sid El Gomri; or in Kurdistan, where women have their own independent oral traditions.[1]

In women's ritual practice, storytelling plays a major role and takes multiple forms. Although mythic recitations and readings from sacred texts are obvious features of even the most traditional liturgies, worshiping women—both unself-consciously and with deliberate intent—have embraced narrative to a unique degree. Storytelling seems to resonate with women's instinctive methods of communication: personal anecdote, neighborhood news related over the backyard fence, an impulse toward analogy and metaphor, stories told to sleepy children, the easy sharing of deep confidences, the intergenerational transfer of the mysteries and lore of womanhood.

Reflection on women's ritualizing recognizes this yearning toward the telling of tales. Ruether repeatedly recommends sharing personal accounts in the suggested rites in *Women-Church*. Barbara Walker has outlined a number of women's rituals that depend on storytelling; among them are rites for celebrating heroines, reading and elaborating myths of the goddess, and "storetelling," Walker's term for retelling old tales without their patriarchal content.[2] In the contemporary literature of feminist liturgy, both descriptive and critical, the theme of narrative is also a constant refrain. Charlotte Caron notes that "feminist theological/thealogical method begins with *the telling of women's stories.*"[3] Liturgy-maker Dianne Neu, discussing women's ritualizing, identifies narrative not only as a ritual element but as the mode of the discussion itself.[4]

Types of Narrative

The narrative techniques employed by women are many and varied, ranging from the personal and spontaneous to the formal and structured; they fall into a number of formal categories.

Autobiography

The most noticeable and discussed of these categories is autobiography. When women gather to worship, perhaps the single most common ritual element is the narration of personal stories. These may be incorporated in a variety of forms: casual reminiscences, vivid tales of pain for which healing is requested, sharings on a chosen theme, stories prepared specifically to fulfill some ritual purpose, spontaneous interjections and responses, and so on.

Whatever form it takes, autobiographical material serves a number of critical functions in women's ritualizing. First, telling women's stories allows the recitation of women's history, redressing (at least symbolically) the egregious omission of women's experiences and contributions from the conventional historical record, especially in sacred texts, and asserting the importance of the stories of "ordinary" people to the collective myth.

Second, getting in touch with and relating stories of their own lives is often a cathartic experience for participating women. As even a cursory investigation of Pentecostal, charismatic, and possession religions demonstrates, catharsis is a powerful experience that often opens the worshiper to new dimensions of spiritual awareness as it releases guilt, fear, expectation, and/or pain. For many women, the constrictions of culture or of traditional religions have made authentic spiritual experience difficult, if not impossible. Recounting personal episodes or chronologies frequently allows the deepening of relationships, both within the gathered community and with the sacred.

Third, autobiography can be a powerful motivator for religious response and ethical action within a worshiping community. Hearing the stories of those who have suffered or triumphed, lost or discovered faith, isolated themselves or blossomed can inspire commitment, lead to empowerment, and build solidarity—resulting in a stronger religious group and in the potential for meaningful social activity on behalf of others.

Fourth, autobiographical stories can serve as models for behavior, spirituality, and ritualizing. Tales of a founder, such as Mother Anderson of the New Orleans Spiritual Church, not only solidify the group myth but also provide exemplary patterns to be followed. Stories of individuals who have overcome adversity, achieved despite oppressive circumstances, or demonstrated spiritual power inspire courage, hope, and emulative behavior.

Finally, in a ritualizing context, autobiographical narrative may provide an educational function, tracing the history of the group or of women more generally, offering a description and analysis of patriarchal realities, investigating theological questions, and otherwise making religious practice intelligible and acceptable to women worshipers.

Although autobiography constitutes a rich mine of ritual meaning for women, Sered offers a caveat. Making the point that women's religious autobiographies are just that—personal experiences tempered both by their religious context and by the fact that they are told by women—she notes that autobiography is not coterminous with fact. Rather, women's religious stories are interpreted stories, arranged in narrative form (as opposed to the random and chaotic patterns of real life), edited for relevance, told from a particular point of view, and invested with religious significance.[5] As such, they go beyond mere description and become part of a larger theological enterprise.

Testimony. Testimony, while being singularly personal, nonetheless demonstrates the common threads in women's narrative. Religious testimony is not, of course, the exclusive province of women, but some research demonstrates that it takes unique forms among them. Elaine Lawless, for example, discusses the experience of women's call to preach in the Pentecostal tradition and their testimonies to that call. Noting that "the stories are very similar, even from women who might never have met," she outlines a particular narrative structure peculiar to this genre: a dismaying call from God, resistance to it, a test of God's presence and activity, rejection by the community, and subsequent itinerancy. Responding to a series of self-imposed questions regarding the peculiarity of women's concerns, approaches, and narrative style, she concludes that preaching, as well as the testimonial form, are indeed gender-defined.[6]

In one of New Orleans' African American Spiritual churches, the feast of Queen Esther assumes great importance as a ceremony of protest and self-esteem for women. Many women testify on that occasion to the influence of their patronal spirit on their lives, thanking her for gifts of money or jobs, praising her role as spiritual guide and mediator, and recognizing her as an inspiration and source of courage for women, as well as a model of bravery and boldness.[7] This use of testimony—for personal empowerment and affirmation—appears to be a functional adaptation peculiar to women.

Fulkerson also discusses testimony as a narrative form with particular value for women. She outlines three kinds of religious testimony: accounts of blessings received, personal reminiscences of God's effect on the narrator's life, and homiletic testimonies. Again looking at Pentecostal women (for whom testimony is a familiar and comfortable experience), she notes that the second type—personal reminiscence—dominates women's testimonial reports. She goes on to comment that these forms are most appropriate to the oral mode of communication, which often suffuses women's ritualizing. Moreover, she notes, "the stories do important work for the teller," serving as self-assurances in an insecure world; indeed, "they deploy ideas about [women's] worthlessness and their submission to authorities through themes of victory and remarkable accomplishment. Through the stories, they tell who they are."[8]

Sociologist Wade Clark Roof remarks that testimony is an old form of religious narrative that seems to be once again gaining in popularity. He attributes this to the attraction of subjective religious experience and personally interactive ritual forms. The emphasis on the individual and private, however, is only part of the picture; even more important may be the way in which testimony recapitulates the experience of the larger community: "In testimony, a person's own religious story becomes linked to a larger story of hope and salvation; the believer finds meaning for his or her life in a larger narrative."[9] Although Roof is not reflecting specifically on gender concerns, this observation highlights the values that make testimony a crucial form of narrative for ritualizing women.

Storytelling and Myth

Autobiography (or autobiographical testimony), prevalent as it is in women's ritualizing (and correspondingly absent in more familiar forms of worship), is only one kind of narrative. Still, it is integrally connected with storytelling of all kinds, especially with the stories of other individuals and the stories of communities. Telling a story of self opens up possibilities for hearing and understanding the stories of others, because "our story is not simply our internal story, it is constituted by others' stories as well."[10] Moreover, an autobiographical tale "invites one to tell one's own personal and collective stories in response. Stories evoke other stories."[11] Thus, the sharing of personal biography leads to a chain reaction in which the collective story of the community—its myth—is developed.

Stories do not always arise out of individual autobiography. In fact, quite the opposite is sometimes true: community stories shape our own. As William G. Doty observes, "We are our stories. We become our stories." Calling personal stories "contemporary mythologies," Doty goes on to note that "sometimes these stories are taken from the communal imaginings that have been disciplined for public sharing."[12] The community, too, has a biography that comprises the body of personal experiences brought to it by its members, as well as the larger story that represents the communal myth—whether it is a myth of explanation, spiritual connection, corporate origins, sociological functionality, or psychological modeling.

It is not only, however, the content of these recitations that shapes the community story; the telling itself is the principal agent of the transformation from mere story to evolving myth. James B. Wiggins notes that "the importance of stories lies ultimately less in what is told than in how whatever is told gets told."[13] Taking this idea further, Michael Novak asserts plainly that story *is* method, that its function is to articulate a change in experience, especially the kind of experience that fundamentally alters one's context and "horizon."[14]

Storytelling accomplishes this core realignment by its power as a performative utterance—that is, by being itself and constituting a new view of reality in the very act of being breathed into existence. Moreover, like any efficacious symbol set, it invites relationship and interpretation, promising to yield meaning. It is never "only a story," but comprises both the narrative content and the interpretive process incorporated into it each time it is retold.[15] Demonstrating no simple one-to-one correspondence with its interpretations and incapable of being exhausted by them, it nonetheless evokes ever deeper layers of engagement and response, opening new vistas of understanding and possible action in those who participate, whether as listeners or speakers.[16]

As a mythmaking and myth-telling device, story serves a particularly poignant purpose for ritualizing women, whose stories have been widely lost or suppressed. In this context, the recounting of personal and community stories becomes the instrument for countering the loss of history and for establishing a new, richer record. Further, in the process, more is created than history, as the community develops its unique mythology. As does all good myth, the narrative process creates for ritualizing women models for living authentic lives.[17]

Prayer

Marjorie Procter-Smith asks whether the needful establishment of a corpus of stories can serve as more than history or myth—specifically, whether it can provide a channel for direct relationship with the divine. Her reasoning begins with an acknowledgment that a story is addressed to the community, but, not surprisingly, she defines a community in which the sacred is immanent and experienced in the gathering itself. Thus, she concludes, "telling one's story in the community is telling it to God," and talking to "God" is the definition of prayer.[18] Insofar as telling stories also makes the sacred present to others, the stories themselves take on the quality of divinity.

In many religions, the sort of dialogue that establishes story as prayer also sets roles and authority. The Korean shaman, for example, engages in a continual form of give-and-take with her congregation, a feature most evident in Western religion, perhaps, in the call-and-response homiletic style of African American preachers. Dialogue appears in the tradition of auricular confession common to various Christian churches. Clearly, the dialogic character of storytelling is not unique to women's ritualizing, but it may serve rather different purposes in that context than it has in more conventional religious settings. Most notably, women's ritual dialogue functions less to fix and enforce lines of authority than to draw participants into relationship, particularly with one another as individuals and/or as conduits of sacredness.

Sacred Texts

> The bookseller called to the people in the village:
> "Story books for women, sacred books for men.
> Story books for women, sacred books for men."
> > —from the movie *Yentl*
> The bookseller didn't know what women have discovered:
> the stories are what make the books sacred.[19]

The traditional aversion in Western religions to understanding the Bible and other sacred texts as stories, or even as myth, has created the popular dichotomy expressed by the bookseller: stories—that is, fictional and untrue fantastic tales—are the appropriate province for women, whereas men alone can tackle the serious, profoundly meaningful communications that arrive direct from the deity.

The editorial comment from *Ruach,* however, points to a deeper truth—namely, that stories are the point; stories are sacred; indeed, that stories are what make texts valuable.

Sacred texts are a form of religious narrative so critical to the Western mindset that it is difficult to imagine religion without them. The lengthy process of oral recitation that preceded the production of written texts is equally opaque to us, and it is easy to forget that generation upon generation told stories before those tales became codified in books believed, ages after the first tellers were gone, to be written by the hand of God.

The inherited texts of the Semitic religions so clearly omit the stories of women that ritualizing women must recreate them and start over. It may be that future generations will adopt texts that comprise the oft-retold stories of women that are just now being reclaimed and remembered, but in contemporary women's spirituality, there are no sacred texts. Certain texts—say, the writings of the suffragists, women's poetry, or the recovered autobiographies of women in earlier ages—may also eventually attain semisacred status. Many of these are already incorporated into rituals performed by women and provide significant spiritual sustenance.

Because of the unquestionable link between narrative and texts, critiques of women's use of stories frequently issue a warning against the textualization of ritual, "the emergence of authoritative textual guidelines," as Catherine Bell puts it.[20] She notes that such textualization can also produce the codification of dogma, bureaucratization, institutionalization, and tensions between hierarchies and local custom. Although traditional liturgiologists may fret, with Aidan Kavanagh, that "any ritual without 'canon' . . . is no ritual at all,"[21] ritualizing women, in both older religions and contemporary groups, appear to be avoiding, thus far, the temptation to elevate stories to canonical status. The possibility remains, however, that in recovering women's history, they will be tempted to follow the Western scriptural model in establishing the centrality of the resulting texts.

Nonetheless, it does not seem that worshiping women lean toward the production of such texts or that they are comfortable relying on them. The ritualization process itself, with its dynamic, spontaneous, and responsive emphases, guards against the formalization of texts that might, with use over time, accrue to themselves authority gleaned at the expense of the gathered assembly. Contemporary women, many of whom first discovered a sense of solidarity with other spiritual women by recognizing that Western scriptures were skewed as reportage and damaging as norms, appear to be wary of the dangers of letting stories become petrified into texts and letting texts become enshrined as absolute truth.

Even in older religions dominated by women, texts play a relatively small part, and traditional scripture in Christian sects is quickly supplemented with the stories and personal insights of women founders (Ann Lee, Mary Baker Eddy) or prophets (Leafy Anderson, Myrtle Fillmore). In non-Western women's religions, texts play such a small part that Sered is able to say rather categorically that women's religions are characterized by a lack of authoritative sacred texts,[22] despite the general literacy of the societies in which these religions occur. And though she comments that the feminist spirituality movement has produced a great number of books, none of these pretend to sacred status. In fact, Sered finds it surprising that, given the highly literary character of the movement, there is no official scripture, or even any discernible movement toward creating one.

Uses of Narrative

How narrative is used is as significant as what it contains. Fulkerson notes that feminist theologians often ascribe power to language "by means of semantic meanings or textual features as they are *used* against women."[23] She goes on to suggest that use determines meaning and that words and texts can assume different meanings as social locations change. Given this assumption, the reluctance of ritualizing women to codify their texts is understandable. Moreover, we should expect that narrative texts, written or performed, fulfill a wide range of purposes and convey unlimited potential for meaning in women's worship. Those uses, as discussed below, are variously pragmatic, spiritual, or political.

History. A major project of feminism in the 1970s was the construction of women's history through the recordation of women's biographical and autobiographical stories. Whereas Judaism, Christianity, and Islam find identity in their claim to being historical and narrative, it became clear to many women that such linear narratives can be and have been subject to editorial revision and omission. What is missing, on the whole, are the stories of ordinary people, particularly of women, in what Arthur Schlesinger calls "the most spectacular casualty of traditional history."[24] As I have mentioned, ritualizing women redress this failed historical recordation by telling their own stories and those of women who have gone before, constructing a new narrative and a new way of doing history.

It must be noted that not all feminists agree on the appropriateness of this historical strategy. Jane Lewis argues that in historical research, "both methodologically and in terms of its (limited) effect on the writing of history more generally, this approach was no longer making waves by the 1980s."[25] Angela McRobbie has remarked on the particular use of oral history, which she perceives as "parasitic on women's entrapment in the ghettos of gossip."[26] Nonetheless, ritualizing women of all persuasions generally seem to agree that "women's experiences are historical, rather than ontological," and they are using that understanding as a basis for ritual activity.[27]

Remembrance. Closely connected with the historical element of ritualized narrative is its use as remembrance, in keeping with the traditional understanding that "the telling of stories is deeply linked with the wellsprings of memory, and women are the keepers of the flame."[28] This approach has been most fully developed by Elisabeth Schüssler Fiorenza in the context of biblical hermeneutics. Her concern is "how to write women into history," in light of their absence from traditional texts.[29] The "subversive memory" that she identifies and seeks to invoke through an imaginative reclamation of the past surfaces in women's ritualization as, among other things, "stories of women which reconstruct the past and shape the future."[30] For women who choose to remain within the classical religious traditions, this is a crucial task: "As we tell the texts of our lives, slowly we find that our stories are resonant of a legacy that stretches back to the beginning of time."[31]

Elizabeth Ozorak points out that the salient characteristic of memory is that it preserves meaning, not that it preserves facts.[32] Procter-Smith contextualizes this as the quality of "secrecy" inherent in women's remembering, a forced necessity in oppressive circumstances. For her, there is little distinction between "secret" and "lost," between deliberate and unintentional suppression of the factual details of events; what must be remembered is the lessons they convey.[33] Ritualizing women reclaim religious significance through the stimulation of creative memory and the conscious awareness of the importance of keeping stories—not facts—alive. What results is a social memory that is particularly important for feminists, who "locate themselves and their political actions in the larger social order in accordance with the sets of meanings that they have learned by listening to other women's stories."[34]

Self-construction. Telling stories allows the teller to construct an outline, to understand her own experience, to become real. Narratives, Linda Sexson tells us, "are not only reflective but also formative. We create the universe as we go along, evolving, by flesh and by story. . . . We construct our lives by our story construction."[35] This is especially evident when ritualizing women share with others autobiographical stories that would remain untold and hidden in any other context.[36]

Community Construction. The particularities of a narrative allow its telling to function as an act of self-construction, yet at the same time the story reveals commonalities that, in the context of a ritualizing group, help form community. Although "what one most desperately wants to discover in one's life story is not that the story is everyone's story," nonetheless "one longs to discover the universal dimensions embodied in one's story."[37] Beyond the aggregating quality of sharing and mutual discovery, the story, which may begin as a tale of personal experience, becomes part of the larger story of the community at worship. Not only are we involved with the other personae in our story, but we are also drawn into relationship with those with whom we experience the storytelling itself.

Testimonial. Part of the power of narrative to form community, as is discussed earlier, is inherent in its nature as testimony, as witnessing to and witnessing by. Testimony both reveals the forces that frame gender definition and women's experience and makes truth claims that burden and emancipate the community.[38] Telling stories as testimony creates a contractual communal commitment to restructure the power relations at the heart of ritual.

Myth. In ritually telling their stories, women participate in the creation of myth, as they have from time immemorial. In many cultures, women are the keepers of the myths, a role reemphasized today as women ritualize together. To claim that women's particular stories are myths themselves would be dubious at best, as Diane Purkiss has pointed out; nonetheless, she suggests that "such domestications can be read as powerfully strategic disruptions."[39] Contemporary ritualizing women use narrative in part to reconstruct a constitutive story that disrupts and challenges traditional myth while recognizing the power of mythical representation.

Healing. Despite Sexson's caveat that "stories are not recipes, not therapy,"[40] there can be no denying the therapeutic effect of much of women's ritualized storytelling. Within the constructed safety and ritual structure of women's communal worship, narrative has both external and internal functions, reflecting the tension of the communal and the particular that pervades women's ritualizing. Inherent in the freewheeling, nontextual nature of narrative in such settings is the possibility of the shared confidence, the keening wail, the cry for help:

> Women need to say what life is really like—to tell the truth about their lives. In rituals, women talk about traumas, pain, suffering, and joys, and they celebrate the milestones in relationships, work situations, the creation of home environments, and spiritual discoveries. For example, at one ritual three women spoke about work—one was quitting an unfulfilling job to start a business of her own; the second was exhausted from a hard day at work; another, with no resources to live on, was desperately looking for a job. Another night, four women talked about what it is like to be getting older in an ageist society. Others told of experiences of violation, sexual abuse, and incest as they sought healing. Another woman spoke of how being part of feminist rituals had allowed her to shift her priorities from money to enjoyable work.[41]

Storytelling can effect not only psychological healing but spiritual healing as well. As Mary Grey notes, "Stories have the power to set in motion a process of *metanoia*, of repentance and reconciliation."[42] Not only can this process lead to a reconnection with the sacred in the lives of worshiping women, but it can also offer hope amid oppression and a method for reconciling with the larger society.

Reflection. Of all the elements common to women's ritualizing, perhaps the most distinctive and, especially in feminist groups, the most pervasive is narrative reflection on the ritual as part of the ritual process itself. Grimes somewhat cynically notes that reflexivity as a ritual element has been a common theme of postmodernism, which makes him "suspicious of it when it begins to sound like a criterion or value."[43] Without elevating it to a form of idolatry, however, ritualizing women have internalized reflexivity into the ritual itself as part of a nonhierarchical approach to ritual generation and an acknowledgment that the process supersedes the product.

Women's Ritualizing and Narrative Theory

In reevaluating the long Western religious tradition of a purely textual (that is, scriptural) employment of narrative, liturgical revision—a quintessentially modernist phenomenon—along with Christian and Jewish feminist liturgical theory, has found itself comfortably in sync with the emphasis on narrative necessity and efficacy that is typical of ritual theorists such as Victor Turner and the deconstructionists. Indeed, it is probably true, as Ron Grimes says, that "the terms 'narrative' and 'story' are exercising an almost incantatory sway over the field of religious studies" at this time.[44]

Grimes identifies six "clusters" of thought within the larger category of narrative theology: sacred biography, faith development, psychobiography, character and community, biblical narrative, and myth and ritual (focused on explicating classic texts). This schema, although fairly comprehensive, yields no area that can be said to include the development of narrative that has taken place in women's spiritual communities. It might be suggested that narrative, consciously employed as a strategy of feminist liturgical theology, should constitute a seventh field on Grimes's list.

That feminist ritualizing privileges narrative is evident not only in its encouragement of the telling of both personal and historical stories, but also in its stress upon narrative (rather than performative) reflexivity. Reflexivity in a ritual context implies a certain dependence on, at least, a narrative structure or content. Various theorists have posited reflexivity as a crucial condition of self-construction, a position that Grimes finds untenable and even dangerous.[45] He even suggests, following Mary Wakeman, that a narrative approach to self-construction is inherently patriarchal.[46] However, the reflexivity cultivated as an essential element of women's ritualizing centers principally on process; its stress is on community formation, egalitarian expression, recognition of the other in the act of reflection, and continuous ritual re-creation. As such, it largely avoids the "narcissism" identified by Richard Schechner and others as at the core of the postmodern era.

Although narrative theology and theory are still a hot item in the study of religion generally, the spell is weakening in ritual studies, into which the postmodern influence in cultural studies is increasingly filtering. Yet despite feminist theory's condemnation of modernity and general embrace of difference and particularity, elements of postmodernism specific to ritual—especially the understanding of symbol and meaning as nonfoundational and unidentifiable outside a given situation—have had only a limited impact on the theory of women's ritualizing. Likewise, attempts to eliminate subjectivity have found inhospitable ground there; after all, "only subjective agents who have some degree of consciousness of themselves as such can possibly struggle for freedom."[47]

Because women's ritualizing does not posit reflection as a category in opposition to ritual practice but has ritualized reflexivity itself, it has avoided (or at least circumvented) the reflection-thought-narrative/performance-action duality elaborated by many postmodernists. Grimes, who likes setting up typologies, sees narrative and ritual as opposing categories, a perception informed by his equation of narrative with text and ritual with performance.[48] Despite their emphasis on narrative, however, when women ritualize, performance—even of the most spontaneous sort—is hardly slighted; dance and other kinds of movement, tactile interaction with a variety of objects, nonlinguistic utterance (moaning, chanting, crying out, and the like), dramatic presentations, and an as yet uncanonized panoply of ritual acts are perhaps the hallmark of women's worship.

Narrative in this context, then, is also performative; beyond the simple telling of stories, it may include the enactment of feelings, occasions, and experiences through a wide range of performative techniques. Singularly absent from most women's ritual events are canonical or prescriptive texts, and the liturgies themselves are generally ad hoc and transitory. Although structures may be repeated or built upon, ritualizing women implicitly try to avoid the transition of rituals into rites.

Thus, although women's ritualizing may seem comfortably ensconced in the narrative theology camp, it has clear affinities—especially in its stress on particularity, difference, and performance—with postmodern cultural and literary theory. And although much recent ritual theory has tended to pit narrative and performance against each other, women's worship tends to overcome this duality, as Grimes has suggested, by predicating narration in relation to enacting and unifying temporality with spatiality in the physical performance and response to storytelling.[49]

Narrative Insight into Ritualizing

Although feminist theorists in general, and feminist liturgiologists more specifically, have paid little attention, on the whole, to the role of narrative in women's ritualizing, descriptions and observations of what women actually do in such situations tell another story, so to speak. Women's spiritual gatherings are replete with narratives of all kinds: autobiographical sharings, bits of ancient myth, stories told through song and dance and mime, neglected scriptural pericopes, legends of the goddess, literal old wives' tales, testimonies, parables.

Indeed, narrative is at the heart of how women understand themselves, express themselves, and create community among themselves. As Caron remarks, "Women's stories must be told. Women's voices must be heard in all aspects of life, culture, politics, and religion. Women must be able to go deep within and to articulate freely the concerns, experiences, hopes, and fears that are real."[50] Ritualizing women have taken that narrative emphasis and rescued it from the excessive linearity and tradition-dependence of the classical religions, imbuing it with a particularity and a spontaneity that mark it as a cutting-edge insight into ritual behavior.

ritualizing the politics of women's ritualizing

*the politics of women's ritualizing the politics of
women's ritualizing the politics of women's ritualizing*

Creative ritualizing has allowed women in a variety of cultures to more fully articulate and reenvision their religious experiences. In many instances, it has also provided a mechanism for social critique and renovation. Ritual expression and action can be, and often are, political expression and action. The connection of ritual and politics is neither tenuous nor transitory; for example, ritual is almost a sine qua non in civil (political) ceremony of all kinds. One need only study the ritual genius of Adolf Hitler to confirm the extent to which ritual can be put to the service of political aims, however grim.

The connection of religion and politics through the medium of ritual may seem less obvious but is also easily supported. The ability of the Christian conservative movement to mobilize voters, the ritualization of antichoice campaigning by the Roman Catholic Church, the force consolidated in an Islamic jihad or in the Christian Crusades—a limitless array of instances demonstrate the power of religious movements to exert social as well as dogmatic control using ritual means to gain and unify support, evoke powerful images, create solidarity, and stimulate action.

Carrying the linkage one step further connects politics, ritualizing, and women's religious activity. This is perhaps most obvious when considered in relation to feminist spirituality. Feminism's early roots as a movement for women's equal treatment were specifically political, and they have only been manifested in the development of specifically feminist religious forms relatively recently. Yet those forms echo classic feminist theory. If, for feminists, the religious can be political, a quick review of the elements enumerated in chapter 2—which emphasize the ordinary, the domestic, the emotional—reinforces the feminist truism that the personal is political.

The political ramifications of women's ritualizing reach beyond intentionally feminist communities to women's groups with earlier origins and to those in non-Western cultures. There are vast differences among these religious groups in how they engage the social order in dialogue, how they understand their goals, and how they ritualize statuses, roles, and aspirations. Many do not acknowledge any political intent behind their ritual activity—a red flag for Western social scientists who too facilely presume they know more about what is actually going on in the rituals of other cultures than do the ritual participants themselves.[1] Even assuming, however, that nonfeminist women's religious groups, being unconscious of any political motivations, are therefore free of them, and allowing for the particularities of time, place, and culture, there still emerges a greater predilection for social critique in women's worship than is generally associated with other religious rituals.

Ritualizing as Constitutive

Ritualization can function as a powerful political tool because of its ability not only to reflect but also to construct various aspects of social reality. This capacity is fairly obvious in religious settings; to use a familiar example, a minyan of Jewish worshipers at a synagogue service does not just represent but also constitutes the whole Jewish people. Similarly, in the "liturgical" Christian tradition, the consecrated bread and wine of the mass is not a mere reminder of the life of Jesus but constitutes his actual presence in a specific time and place. What is true for these familiar traditions is equally applicable to other religions. Writing on Yoruba practices, Margaret Drewal notes that "rituals operate not merely as models *of* and *for* society that somehow stand timelessly alongside 'real' life. Rather, they construct what reality is and how it is experienced and understood."[2]

This ability of ritual to create what is understood to be authentic reality operates on various levels. On the one hand, a community of like-minded members may use ritual to define what is "really real" within the context of its own practice and belief. Such a closed system allows the group to create an alternative reality to that of the outside world, at least during the enactment of the appropriate rituals—though often it is understood to obtain perpetually. This more perfect alternative both testifies against the failed and flawed external society and provides a refuge from it. On the other hand, a group may use, or attempt to use, ritual to affect directly the social order outside the confines or authority of the community itself; the ritual protests of the 1960s and 1970s, for example, went beyond the immediate community of college life, aiming successfully to excite and involve other participants, to challenge the established system, to explore new approaches to morality and ethics and, ultimately, to effect changes in national policy.[3]

The constitutive power of ritual casts a wide net, but several of its fields of influence are particularly relevant to this discussion. First among these is the ability of ritual to construct, enhance, and enable personhood. The most obvious form this takes is psychological; ritual performance can "articulate the deepest currents hidden in people's lives and, in this, help people to realize who they are. In another sense, ritual provides a person with a way of expressing one's self-worth."[4] Thus, ritual provides one way for humans to get more deeply in touch with their sense of self.

Personal growth, however, can also be understood as the starting point for political awareness, since "ritual gives us a sense of being a participant rather than a pawn in life's drama."[5] What is more, ritual, with its inherently communal quality, can further move a person toward social attunement. Ritualizing people are people in community, operating in a society with norms, values, and expectations. David Kertzer notes that "through ritual the individual's subjective experience interacts with and is molded by social forces."[6] Not only the experience but also the person herself is thus molded. It is no accident that the early leaders of the women's suffrage movement learned the arguments and the tools they needed for political success in the church schools and offices where they participated in weekly rituals. This learning process involves, among other things, the acquisition of symbolic language and knowledge of its uses. Kertzer makes the point that the medium of political discourse is symbol, as it is of ritual;[7] familiarity with ritual techniques breeds political understanding as well as religious expression.

If indeed rituals are, in part at least, constitutive of persons, they are also—and more dangerously—involved in the construction of categories of persons.[8] In today's pluralistic milieu, in both the East and the West, the rituals of a group of people often are the most public and perhaps the most fundamental aspect of the group's identity. A sect, an ethnic community, or a social class may well be defined and recognized primarily by its ritual behaviors, including such factors as its dress, gesture, and cuisine, as well as its formal ceremonies.

By extension, rituals also construct hierarchies within these communities; that is, rituals can provide the means for isolating, stratifying, and relativizing social groups. Bell reflects that although "expedient systems of ritualized relations" advance social integration, as Durkheim famously claimed, they also "are concerned with distinguishing local identities, ordering social differences, and controlling the contention and negotiation involved in the appropriation of symbols."[9] Bruce Lincoln puts this succinctly:

> Ritual, etiquette, and other strongly habituated forms of practical discourse and discursive practice do not just encode and transmit messages, but they play an active and important role in the construction, maintenance, and modification of the borders, structures, and hierarchic relations that characterize and constitute society itself.[10]

The mechanism for this process, as described by Bell, is deceptively simple: rituals appropriate elements of the shared culture, incorporate them into ritual activity, and, by doing so, influence participants who then deploy them in new cultural contexts.[11] Thus, preexisting and possibly dormant cultural features are adapted through the ritual medium into powerful shapers of cultural identity, status, and significance.

These processes of cultural construction are, clearly, available to women. Indeed, women are engaged in them all the time. As Procter-Smith notes, "Women can and do create culture; what is critical is that we recognize the political act inherent in creating culture."[12] For her, the recognition itself is the principal benefit of specifically feminist ritual; women need to be more aware of their ability to construct an alternative social reality through ritual means. Chris Smith echoes this concern, saying that "our spiritual lives are in desperate need of rituals that weave the political and the religious together as one fabric."[13] Although this understanding may not be fully articulated in all cultures, the power to participate in the ritual constitution of society—through zar cults, for example, or spirit channeling—appears to have been frequently and skillfully appropriated by women in a variety of circumstances.

Ritual, Discourse, and Power

The era of cultural criticism has broadened the meaning of the term "discourse," allowing a fuller understanding of the ways in which we communicate with one another. Far more than a mere exchange of language, discourse encompasses the full range of media—costume, movement, visual arts, architecture, performance, rhetoric, song, and so on—that allow human interaction and the transference of information or meaning. In this sense, ritual behavior is a significant form of discourse, communicating some aspect of ultimate meaning, providing data about the identity and ideology of the group performing it, and often issuing a persuasive appeal for new participants, public support, or a particular course of action.

Discourse, in turn, is directly related to the assumption and use of power. Power, as defined in Saul Alinsky's classic handbook for dissent, *Rules for Radicals*, is "the ability, whether physical, mental, or moral, to act."[14] This definition is probably as useful as any other. Lincoln clarifies that this potential to act involves the implication of some sort of superior strength: "No consideration of discourse is complete that does not also take account of force." For him, discourse, particularly in the form of ideological persuasion, supplements force as a coercive phenomenon that "may be strategically employed to mystify the inevitable inequities of any social order and to win the consent of those over whom power is exercised, . . . transforming simple power into 'legitimate' authority."[15]

Obvious examples of this truism abound in the arena of civil ritual, from the tactics deployed in any campaign for public office to, as a specific example, the manipulation of public opinion by the shrewd and ritualized use of Generals Colin Powell and Norman Schwarzkopf during the Persian Gulf War. One could validly, if somewhat cynically, suggest that precisely the same thing occurs in some familiar worship services, where music, preaching, and healing are used to produce highly emotional responses and dependencies, as well as a concomitant deep commitment to the leadership structure of the community.

Neither is the academic community immune to the allure of a certain kind of scholarly discourse that reinforces existing power systems. Henry Pernet highlights, for example, the androcentrism that has dominated anthropological research, discussing

[the] "male complicity" that is apparent in a number of old texts in which the anthropologist (male) does not doubt for a second the information with which his informants (also male) supplied him. . . . Obviously proud to be let in on the secrets of his informants, the anthropologist completely loses his critical faculties.[16]

Later scholars, Pernet notes dryly, easily exposed the exaggeration of male superiority that resulted from this bias. Many today might question the implication that this was solely a problem with earlier researchers. In any event, academic power (certainly a ritualized commodity) has been used—or in this case, misused—to produce a convincing, if erroneous, portrait of social relations in a given culture that, by theoretical extension, can also affect the culture of the anthropologist himself.

If discourse is power and ritual is discourse, logic leads to the inescapable conclusion that ritual is—or at least is largely about—power. This is the essence of Bell's presentation:

> Ritualization *is* very much concerned with power. Closely involved with the objectification and legitimation of an ordering of power as an assumption of the way things really are, ritualization is a strategic arena for the embodiment of power relations.[17]

In the work of almost all the seminal scholars in the area of ritual studies, the issue of ritual as a form of social control continually arises; Durkheim, Turner, Bellah, Gluckman, Girard, and others have hypothesized the function of ritual in creating, stabilizing, and maintaining societies and their power structures.[18] There is general agreement that ritual performs extremely useful purposes for dominant groups, mystifying the current order (as Lincoln would have it) and thus making it appear transcendent, inevitable, and worthy of assent. A familiar parable on this theme is presented (discursively) in the film and stage play *Evita*, which dramatically demonstrates the capacity of ritualized discourse to support and extend power structures.

Women, however, are not generally found among the power elite, Eva Perón notwithstanding. Nowhere does women's ritualizing reflect a consciousness that women are currently dominant. Ritual in this context must, consequently, be able to serve the function of challenging existing power structures and providing access to the mechanisms of social control—or at least social equity.

As Lincoln remarks, power isn't the exclusive province of the elite, and "nondominant groups of all sorts always retain some measure of force—if only that of their own bodies."[19] The power of such groups lies principally in their ability to disrupt, "demystify, delegitimate, and deconstruct the established norms, institutions, and discourses that play a role in constructing their subordination."[20] They can achieve this, according to Lincoln, by refusing to participate in the current order, by overthrowing those in power, or by fundamentally reshaping social patterns. Their success, he continues, depends on whether they can gain an effective hearing, disseminate persuasive discourse, and succeed in recruiting a following.[21] In summary, he writes, "Those discourses that disrupt previously persuasive discourses of legitimation and those that mobilize novel social formations by evoking previously latent sentiments of affinity or estrangement are among the most powerful instruments of social change."[22]

Applied to ritualizing women, Lincoln's analysis reads like a political index. Women worshiping together enact a social drama whose purpose, at least subliminally, is precisely to disrupt, demystify, delegitimate, and deconstruct both some institutional religious forces and the social structures they create and fortify. Although these essentially political goals might not be consciously deployed, the mere fact that women gather separately to engage in ritualized behavior is a disruptive statement.

For instance, when Christian women gather in groups such as Womenchurch, the gathering poses a series of challenges to the established church: Why do these people feel the need to congregate apart from the rest of the community? What needs are not being met by the established order? Is the older organization seriously flawed? Does the separation imply the possibility of schism? and so on. Such questions force existing institutions to undergo both an implicit and (sometimes) an explicit critique, to accommodate the loss of membership, to risk expansion of a sense of malaise, and to consider the possibility of a need for change. Depending on the cultural forces at work, women's religious groups could similarly confront such entities as male-dominated social structures, governmental agencies, entrenched gender roles, and family patterns, even though the groups' formal activities remain self-contained, with no intentional political motivation.

Ritual and Social Change

Because ritual participates in the actualization of power and the constitution of social relationships, it is a powerful agent for social change. Perhaps the most universal experience of ritual transformation occurs in rites of passage—rituals for major life-cycle events, through which a substantive change can be wrought in social status, role, or identity: the single become married/bonded/under contract; the child becomes a legal adult; the convert becomes a community member; the princess becomes a queen. At such moments, the power of ritual to create change is obvious.

Still, as Grimes points out, the ability of ritual to have "subversive, creative, and culturally critical capacities" was not really recognized until as recently as the 1960s. Grimes attributes this to the 1960s zeitgeist that challenged all fixed assumptions, including the established scholarly notion that ritual was the instrument of the status quo. The instigator of this revised approach, he suggests, was the anthropologist of ritual studies Victor Turner, whose work dominated the field during that period and remains highly influential.[23] On the question of the mutability of rituals, Turner was clear:

> Since I regard cultural symbols including ritual symbols as originating in and sustaining processes involving temporal changes in social relations, and not as timeless entities, I have tried to treat the crucial properties of ritual symbols as being involved in these dynamic developments. Symbols instigate social action.[24]

For Turner, ritual, which operates through symbolic discourse, is specifically an agent of social criticism, change, and action.[25]

In contrast, Bell, despite her equation of ritual with power and her assertion that ritual activity is "a reinterpretation of the world," takes another position. Ritual, she claims, "is *not* a fulcrum for change; it is one of the most conservative media for social action."[26] Indeed, she finds "little justification for seeing ritual as a political medium for quiet revolution in the church or in society."[27] Still, she says, "it is creative, adaptable, and resourceful: constructed with the categories people use to deal with the world, it can give these categories back in schemes more effective for construing the world in ways that envision and empower."[28]

Wade Clark Roof steers a path between these poles, noting that "the role of ritual is complex—it can help to entrench a group's values and make them impervious to change, or it can accelerate those very changes."[29] Ritual both reacts to social change—usually in a protective and conservative mode—and engenders innovative symbolization and models of social reality. The dynamic of ritual and social change works in both directions: although ritual can dampen social alterations, it can also spark them.

Lawrence Hoffman outlines the process by which alterations in the cultural backdrop first initiate small changes in existing rituals; as these accumulate, the community begins to feel distanced from traditional patterns, and the need for further change becomes increasingly evident; eventually, the ritual is discarded, massively revised, or replaced. Then, of course, the new forms themselves inspire new ways of thinking, which in turn spark another round of fine-tuning.[30]

Martha Ellen Stortz takes the dialectic of order and change a step further, suggesting that ritual change be valued not only for its eventual resolution into a more stable order, but also for its own sake:

> Blatant is the assumption that ritual begins and ends in the landscape of structure, with a brief foray into chaos. But what if chaos, plurality, and polyphony could be entertained as values as well? What if ritual were seen both to present and resolve chaos? What if ritual were to begin and end, not only in structure, but in indeterminacy as well?[31]

Such questions, Stortz posits, reveal the possibilities for resistance and subversion that lie with ritual.

In addition to its capacity both to react to social circumstances and to instigate social change, says Kertzer, ritual has yet a third possible function in this regard: it can "systematically misrepresent" the true social situation.[32] In this sense, rituals can misrecord, revise, and edit history—a primary claim of feminist scholars.

Women, Religion, and Ritualizing

The complex relationship of ritual and change is reflected in the efforts of women to find a viable form of expression for their spiritual experiences. Finding ritual in their traditional religions impervious to change—even in fundamental matters such as inclusive language—and suspecting that existing ritual presents a distorted model of and for authentic relationship, they are exploring instead the power of ritual to enable, accelerate, and even create new social constructs.

Sered outlines two models that characterize religions dominated by women. The first tends to reconcile women to their expected social roles, offering only temporary alleviation of their sense of powerlessness; she cites zar practices, which improve a woman's relationship with her husband for a time, as an example. The second model provides a base from which to act collectively for long-term change by building solidarity and networks of influence, economic independence, and women's control of their reproduction.[33] Procter-Smith calls these, respectively, the "sacralizing" (women's roles are seen as sacred) and the "emancipatory" (women's roles can be transcended) functions of women's religions.[34]

In older cultures, the sacralizing model may appear more prominently. Often, the rites controlled by women support the existing social structure but make it more bearable for the participating women by ritualizing their normative behavior, signifying respect for it, or momentarily reversing it. Such religions may seem less challenging to existing norms, largely because they have been in place for some time, but they often, nonetheless, constitute an alternative view of social reality. They may, for example, present a worldview that reorders commonly assumed power relationships or social structures, or subtly encourage women to persevere to achieve or exercise domestic power. By presenting women as respected leaders, they may enhance regard for women's abilities; by providing agencies for solidarity, they may provide support for women's accomplishments or for legal improvements.

In the newer forms of spirituality developing in the modern world, including those influenced by feminism, the challenge to accepted authority is often more blatant, more specific, and more powerfully actualized. There are numerous methods by which women's ritualizing addresses women's social and cultural position and seeks a form of redress.

Unity in Solidarity

One of the most effective political aspects of ritualization is its ability to draw people together into a group, to create community, to communicate common grievances, values, and goals, and to forge the group into a unified force for change. Kertzer, arguing with Durkheim that such solidarity is not only desirable but necessary, summarizes the process succinctly:

> Lacking the formal organization and the material resources that help perpetuate the rule of the elite, the politically deprived need a means of defining a new collectivity. This collectivity, created through rituals and symbols, not only provides people with an identity different from that encouraged by the elite, but also serves as a means to recruit others to their side.[35]

The source of this solidarity in women's spirituality groups, says Catherine Vincie, is the common experience of voicelessness, a shared history of marginality and oppression, and a shared dream of an alternative future.[36] Finding a voice through ritualization, women can come together despite their particular differences and, at least partly through the recitation of their own stories, can develop common goals that reflect their understanding of and sympathy with each other's experiences. Often, the aim of producing a sense of unity can overcome obstacles set up by the established culture, as the women of the Utrecht health collective discovered: "We now understand that the whole talk about women from the 'Third' and the 'First World' being so different is only a trick to keep us separated."[37]

Solidarity can operate in several ways. Sometimes it generates a purely spiritual force. Eko Susan Noble comments that when American Buddhist women unite, "a flow of universal energy comes through our practice and we can use that flow of blessings to aid other beings who are suffering."[38] Sered, using the feminist phrase "Sisterhood is powerful," comments that the more embodied advantages of solidarity include the power to "translate religious participation into secular benefits."[39] Among the obvious benefits are the safety and effectiveness found in numbers, the ability to speak with a louder voice, mutual support in times of crisis or defeat, the intellectual resources to develop a common ideological basis, and the pooling of other resources—money, time, connections, and so on—to support the effort for change.

Group Identity

Closely related to group solidarity is the identity that it helps develop. The need for refurbishing or recreating group identity is especially compelling when social structures are being challenged or altered: "When traditional juridical or ritualistic strategies prove unsatisfactory as modes of redressive action, the group will seek to extricate itself from its dilemma by turning to symbolic action. . . . Ritual serves to coalesce and direct group consciousness."[40] The tug toward unity available in ritual provides an identity based in a shared view of what is "really" real—often in opposition to the social norm—and an alternative to everyday pragmatism and expectations. In this context, the religious community of identity "dares to make the primary definition of what reality is for its members, and it does so, primarily, in its liturgical setting."[41]

Overt Protest

From solidarity, unity, and group identity originates the impetus for social action. Perhaps the most obvious of forms of dissent from the status quo are outright refusal to cooperate, vocal complaint, and pub-

lic debate. Such protest can encourage women to recognize their dis-
comfort with existing situations, provide a gathering point for like-
minded persons, educate other women about their history and options,
and get the attention (and potential support) of the media, the popu-
lace, and the power structure. Kertzer recalls, as an example, that unau-
thorized rituals such as illicit Bastille Day celebrations galvanized the
French Resistance during World War II.[42] Open protest through ritual
activity can uncover what Stortz enumerates as the crucial questions
underlying the presumption that ritual enforces stability and order:
"*Whose* idea of order? *Whose* idea of structure? *Whose* idea of unity?"[43]

Performing Change

The ability to emancipate stems, as Tom Driver notes, from the power
of ritual performance, which "does not *necessarily* resist oppression, but
has a strong potential for doing so. That is because there is no performance without transcendence. If you can perform, you are aware that
you *could* perform differently, and this is the beginning of freedom."[44]
Drewal observes that the process of performing change involves "spontaneous interruptions and interventions in ritual, competitively pulling
and tugging it to shape performance to suit immediate interests and
needs."[45] Performance is action—symbolic action with the power to
effect change.

Confrontation

Some forms of women's spirituality directly challenge prevailing mores.
Although this was not the avowed intent of the Minneapolis Re-Imagining Conference, for example, it clearly was the outcome: established
churches immediately branded the liturgies of the gathering irresponsi-
bly confrontational and sacrilegious. The short-term result was tremen-
dous press coverage and a lot of heated rhetoric; the long-term result,
still to be assessed, may be a heightened awareness of women's needs in
worship.

Another example of the impact of unconventional women's spirituality is cited by Lawrence Babb in his discussion of the Brahma Kumari
movement within Hinduism. Noting that the sect has been, from its
inception, primarily associated with women, Babb draws a clear distinction between general acceptance of women's traditional role as "cus-
todians" of popular Hinduism and the shock that accompanies their
involvement in a celibate movement. As he remarks, "This constitutes a
direct challenge to the prevailing imagery of who women are and what
they should be in the social order."[46]

Providing Solutions for Suffering

According to Sered, "ritual solutions for the problem of suffering in this world are the foci of most women's religions"—a rather sweeping but undeniable statement. "Suffering" can, of course, be broadly defined, but as Sered points out, "given the this-worldly orientation of women's religions, spiritual and earthly benefits tend to be intertwined."[47] Not only have women's religious groups helped women acquire such palliative aids as group support, economic knowledge and growth, spiritual healing, self-esteem, and so forth, but they have also, as Sered says, helped women free themselves from patriarchal thought patterns.

Michael Aune, in contrast, questions whether problem solving is a legitimate function of ritual, calling for "an important shift away from the assumption that the fundamental task of ritual is to 'resolve' basic conflicts or contradictions that have emerged in personal/social life such as those which exist between religious belief and the real world."[48] Assuming that, for ritualizing women, religious belief entails a commitment to equity and mutual respect among persons and in institutional life and that "real life" reiterates patriarchy, Aune's contention would appear unworkable in this case. The ritual activities of women definitely aim to resolve this dichotomy.

Aune's argument leads him to ask, if ritual indeed performs this problem-solving function, would there not be some "reshaping of consciousness, a creating of meaning, and a restructuring of perception of how ritual participants think and feel?"[49] This query, which in the context of traditional religious practice might need to be answered in the negative, reflects precisely the practical political ends and accomplishments of ritualizing women, especially as they seek to redress women's suffering.

Manipulation of Symbols

Rituals, regardless of whether they seek political as well as spiritual ends, depend on symbolic discourse to make an impact on the participants and observers. These symbols are embedded in the myths reflected in and generated by the rituals. Manipulation of the mythical symbols keeps both priests and politicians in business. Lincoln remarks that "change comes not when groups or individuals use 'knowledge' to challenge ideological mystification, but rather when they employ thought and discourse, including even such modes as myth and ritual, as effective instruments of struggle."[50] When the issue is the need for change, the symbols also must change. "The trick," says Kertzer, " is to introduce dramatic variations on these powerful symbols, to change their meaning by changing their context."[51] Thus, to cite an obvious example, bread—used in Christian ceremony to represent the body of Christ, broken to redeem sinners—may become in women's rituals a symbol of women's labor on behalf of family and tribe, and perhaps a representation of the inequities of social compensation and value.

Myth and its constitutive symbols can be used for change, according to Lincoln, in several ways: it can be created from some legend or event, producing a new paradigm for social norms; it can be contested as inauthentic, removing its power to maintain the status quo; or it can be reinterpreted to change its accepted meaning.[52] Ritualizing women, in one forum or another, use all of these options. Within the feminist spirituality community, for example, some exponents argue for a reinterpretation of biblical texts to accommodate the missing stories of women and the patriarchal bias of the record. Others prefer to abandon the old biblical myth, claiming that its inaccuracies deauthorize it. Still others stress developing a new, parallel, and authoritative myth that reclaims women's spiritual history.

Again, Bell voices some caveats about attributing too much power to symbolic activity, citing studies that suggest that symbolic forms, or "rituals of style," work to create group identity but not "politically effective forms of resistance."[53] Although it may be argued that the symbols themselves are not directly effective, in women's spirituality groups the very conscious cultivation of symbolic representations seems to have accomplished more than the building of solidarity. For pagan groups, for instance, casting a circle is understood to be a specifically instrumental act—one with direct repercussions on the surrounding world—rather than merely a sign of unity.

Remembrance

As should be evident by now, memory is a key element in women's religion. Through its imaginative use and stalwart safekeeping, women find and solidify self, community, and ancestry. Memory is created, enlivened, perpetuated, and celebrated in ritualizing. As Mama Lola has discovered, "Consultative ritualizing, like the constant flow of ritual information between New York and Haiti, helps the community guard against forgetting."[54]

But memory is not always comfortable. Beyond its identity-forming function, it also has a political role: "Memory has the potential for resistance, for subversion: interrogating the past leads to questions about the present where women are still not subjects."[55] The temporal continuity of personal and corporate history leads inexorably to the conflicts arising when social advances outstrip cultural adjustments—that is, women's view of their own history is inadequately corroborated in contemporary cultural attitudes. This gap is a powerful motivator for religiopolitical action and change.

Status Reversal

Rituals that reverse the statuses of those in power and those who are not are common in secular life. Once a year, the king acts like a commoner, or washes the feet of a peasant, or is publicly mocked; high school students in a small town are chosen to "run the government" for a day; on certain feasts, men (as in Loiza Aldea in Puerto Rico) dress as women for a wild parade. Such rituals help vent the resentment of the underdogs and advance the political attractiveness of the condescending elite.

This process can also work as part of women's spirituality. Among the Dogon of Africa, for example, women are forbidden to touch the sacred ceremonial masks understood to be the province of men. At the funeral of a woman, however, other women surreptitiously collect fibers from the masks that have fallen during the men's dancing in earlier rituals; with these, they stroke the corpse in a "small symbolic act of consolation, which also constitutes a secret vengeance toward the men." The more knowledgeable men know about this performance but "tolerate it as a legitimate compensation for the type of frustration endured by the women who are kept away from the masks."[56] In the act of death, at least, these women are finally able to transcend the role assigned to them by the male-dominated society in which they live, by reenacting among themselves, with a reversal, the symbolic rites used by the established power structure.

Feminist Religiopolitical Strategies

Unsurprisingly, given the many ways in which women's ritualizing can be a form of political as well as religious expression, some women's groups—especially those that are consciously feminist—have envisioned specific ritual strategies for achieving change in the religiopolitical sphere. Cynthia Eller points out that marginalized groups have available to them two contrasting strategic options in countering cultural assumptions. One, perhaps the more visible option in the earlier days of the feminist movement, argues against those assumptions deemed to be repressive—

such as, to use Eller's example, the negative association of women with nature. From this perspective, many feminists have denied that earthy connection and have promoted an image of women as full participants in the intellectual, technological, asexual world of male religion and power. Many Christian and Jewish feminist groups, for example, have adopted this approach. The other strategic possibility is to embrace the stereotypes imposed by society, insisting that they be positively valued instead. In this instance, Eller remarks, women are proudly accepting their identification with nature and the earth, stressing, in this time of ecological decay, the goodness of women's embodied and earthbound existence and of their commitment to its respect and preservation.[57] This second strategy is evident in, among other instances, goddess and Wiccan worship.

In her earlier writings, Procter-Smith espoused a rather accommodationist approach that promoted women's participation in existing worship systems. In her latest work, however, she sees prayer itself as deeply political, in that it "engages the participants in a web of interlocking assumptions about bodies, communities, God, Jesus (in Christian prayer), human nature, the world, and relationships."[58] Now adopting a more directly confrontational style that grasps women's symbols and ritualizing as inherently good and the notion of disruption as positive, she discusses the Re-Imagining Conference, suggesting that its communion ritual using milk and honey could disrupt and deconstruct traditional eucharistic expectations while nonetheless providing an equivalent sacramentalism. "Whose interests," she asks, "are protected in controlling the content and meaning of Christian eucharistic praying?"[59] Moreover, she suggests, univocal prayer, in which all are expected to speak and respond as one, "creates a coercive space in which consent is assumed and *yes* is the only possible response."[60] For her, then, the only healthy alternative is to reclaim public prayer as a space for saying no to inherited and enforced assumptions, rather than expecting women to acquiesce to a system that devalues their spiritual needs and expression. Challenging traditional rules of performance opens the possibility of devising and interpreting rituals no longer controlled by the hierarchical and marginalizing power structures of the past.

The concept of space is here revealed as critical. When women's ritualizing is perceived as specifically political, space is no longer merely redrawn or resymbolized—it becomes a category and catalyst of change in itself. Thus, Mary Daly argues for a spiritually "new space, in which women are free to become who we are, in which there are real and significant alternatives to the prefabricated identities provided within the enclosed spaces of patriarchal institutions."[61] Redefining space, at least as Daly sees it (or saw it in her earlier work), is a conscious strategy of the second type Ellis describes.

Serene Jones, further refining the notion of reenvisioning liturgical space, suggests that it might be used as a context for examining women's political coalitions. She cautions, however, that if ritual space is to provide a meaningful location for building women's community and furthering their political needs, it must not be too beholden to the notion of natural, rural space as explicitly feminine but must take into account urban space as well; women cannot afford to demonize concrete, highrise technoculture and apotheosize woods and fields without abandoning the vast numbers of women who inhabit urban environments and reflect urban consciousness—certainly not without serious implications for questions of race and class. The ritual space that also comprises political space cannot be idealized or romanticized, she warns, but must take account of brokenness and conflict as well as hope and solidarity.[62]

Myth, too, offers a field for political action within ritualizing. Elizabeth Ozorak, abandoning the attempt to fit circle-defined women into the square hole of traditional patriarchal worship patterns, suggests that women must support and enact "alternative scripts" through the use of new and revised narratives that "instill traits as well as describe them."[63] Wendy Doniger expands on this theme: "Storytellers may, like Judo wrestlers, use the very weight of archetypes to throw them, and with them to throw the prejudices that have colored them for centuries. Call it deconstruction, call it subversion, or just call it creative storytelling."[64] This strategy is effective in helping women to redefine their religious selves positively, to present themselves as strong and outspoken religious leaders, and to understand themselves as crucial actors in the larger story of their faith.

If myth—that is, story—is an appropriate ritual locus for change, then its underlying symbolization also can serve the political needs of ritualizing women. As women manipulate both classic and innovative ritual symbols, they can effect spiritual change as well as a change in institutional consciousness. This transformation, Mary Grey posits, is effected by the vital power of imagination, which "refuses to accept the status quo, and has the creativity to fashion new ways of being."[65] It is this imaginative impulse toward renewal and emancipation that is brought to bear by women worshipers revaluing their place in a spiritual universe.

The Spiritual Dimension of Power

The acquisition of power, in any social sphere, is not generally considered a particularly high-minded motive for action. Whenever women who attain leadership roles in churches refer to women's growing access to the corridors of power, opponents are quick to argue that spirituality is not about power, that God is the only source of power, and that the faithful are called to humility and service. This, of course, is merely a neat way to deflect attention from the core fact that *somebody*, somewhere (and not just God, either) is actually exercising quite a lot of power; and though that somebody or somebodies may display all the outer garb of benign and gentle sheep, there are surely wolves lurking under those vestments. Institutions require the exercise of power and authority to be administered efficiently and to survive. All religions that last eventually become institutionalized. All rely on power structures. For women to acknowledge and seek admittance to those structures is not merely a grab for inessential control but a matter of direct importance to their spirituality; insofar as institutions are understood to mirror the ultimate reality of the sacred, women's place in them is of utmost spiritual importance.

How women exercise the power they gain in religious contexts remains a matter of debate. Sered suggests that women's power is essentially different from that of men: "It is more often personal than positional, it tends to be situationally oriented, and is frequently exercised outside the traditional authority structure of society."[66] These distinctions may be accurate, but they nonetheless reflect a world in which women are excluded from positional, generalized, structured power, not necessarily the incompetence or unwillingness of women to wield that kind of power; that is, they may not represent a uniquely female type of power but merely the type to which women currently have access.

Feminist witch Starhawk also argues that women exercise power differently. She has outlined three levels of power: dominative, charismatic, and "coactive." The first she equates with patriarchy, the second and third with "good" uses of power by women. But Stortz takes issue with this typology, critiquing what she considers a facile and uncritical assumption of feminist ideas by Starhawk, who, she says, is "dismissing dominative power as always coercive and embracing uncritically charismatic and coactive power as liberatory. She ignores the potential positive uses of dominative power, as well as the ambient dangers lurking in charismatic and coactive power."[67]

Stortz argues that the exercise of dominative power—that is, the kind of power to which women have been seeking access in their movement toward leadership and influence in existing churches—is not necessarily antithetical to women's consciousness. Nor is it simply a case of the once-oppressed assuming, upon gaining authority, the same inequitable policies of oppression formerly used against them. Power in and of itself is value-neutral; it is how that power is used that determines its moral status.

Whether women, through their ritualizing, will obtain this sort of power remains to be seen, as do the uses to which they might put it. No doubt the correlative categories of power described by Starhawk and others will also find a place in communities of worshiping women. What does seem clear, however, is that women's ritualizing comprises, in its very nature, a political activity that seeks variously to redress grievances, alleviate suffering, overturn inequity, and elevate the position of women.

ritualizing **the future of women's ritualizing** *the future of women's ritualizing the future of women's ritualizing the future of women's ritualizing the futur*

When they intentionally gather to worship, women tend, as we have seen, to ritualize in distinctive patterns. They draw on an apparently self-selected pool of symbolic themes, texts, objects, and actions; they forge peculiar approaches to the larger issues of sacred space and time; they incorporate various forms of narrative as crucial elements of ritual performance; they seek, find, and develop ritual as a form of political awareness and action. Other commonalities—as well as points of divergence—will emerge as scholars further explore the field. But is women's ritualizing, in fact, a field? Can it be said to constitute a legitimate genre (or subgenre) of academic study? Does it demand and deserve more intensive examination? What, if anything, makes it distinctive?

Women's Ritualizing: Performing Reality

Women's worship is, first and foremost, a performance of perspectives on spiritual and practical reality. As Tom Driver points out, rituals "bear more meanings than words can say. . . . We do not see clear rational meaning but instead the laying out of ways to act, prompted by felt needs, fears, joys, and aspirations."[1] Driver outlines three modes of performance, each of which is evident in women's ritualizing: ritual (dramatic enactment, such as that of the relationship with nature), confessional (related to identity and belief, as in the heavy emphasis on personal narrative), and ethical (concerned with right action—for example, the political aspect of women's worship). He uses the example of women's open-encounter consciousness-raising groups of the 1970s to illustrate confessional performance. (It might be noted that a number of those groups developed into ritualizing groups.) Although, as Driver notes, "under patriarchy women have found it far from easy to perform themselves,"[2] they have found in women's spiritual communities—and not just recently—an important performative locus.

Although discussions of performance theory tend to see ritual action and ritual symbolism as opposing categories, women's ritualizing both acts out old and new realities and suggests ascriptions of meaning to the actions.[3] Not only is it a performance of gender, as Driver implies, but it also functions as cultural performance, generating new meanings and values for the ritualizing society and for the larger culture of which it is a part. Catherine Vincie elaborates that in cultural performance, "the whole community is involved in a demanding ceremony that has as its goal the well-being and betterment of the group."[4]

Ritual performance, as a physical activity, further serves to awaken and stimulate a rich sense of embodiment. As Kay Turner notes, "The body is our first and last outward reality; it defines and conditions our life experience and gives us personal identity and continuity."[5] At the same time that gesture and movement elucidate themselves, they suggest deeper understandings. Here, the conjunction and interdependence of performance and symbolism in women's ritualizing are clearly apparent.

All efficacious ritual performance leads inexorably to transformation. Because ritual is constitutive of reality, it is reality itself that is radically altered. For ritualizing women, what is transformed is primarily the reality of gender, perceived and lived, in both religious and secular contexts. Tom Bremer writes that "the key question [is] how the ritual experience of gender reflects, reiterates, and reinforces gender roles in nonritual contexts and to what degree rituals transform or reconfigure the accepted cultural view and practice of gender."[6] In somewhat different terms, Driver, too, suggests,

What we need today is not the abolition of rituals having to do with sex and power but their transformation or replacement so that newly conceived values in sexual ethics can create pathways along which more just and humane sexual behavior, as we envision it, may go.[7]

Do Women Ritualize Religious Gatherings Only?

To say that women often, when they congregate, worship in patterns peculiar to such gatherings is, of course, not to say that all women ritualize in this way, that all women's rituals are like this, or that all the elements of such ritualizing are unique to women. It does, however, raise the question of whether all women's gatherings are ritualized.

Little attention has been paid by ritual scholars to the dynamics of women's collective activities. Baby showers, quilting bees, afternoon teas, and garden clubs—these and other familiar events have perhaps been overlooked because they seem insignificant, frivolous, devoid of content; that is, they have been treated over the years like most phenomena related to women's lives. Although it is certainly true that many of these activities are playful or meant primarily for amusement, nonetheless, they often bear up to scrutiny as important instances of women's ritualizing.

Dianne Neu's use of the image of quilting to describe women's ritualizing offers one perspective on the relationship of these two creative actions.[8] Another appears in the film *How to Make an American Quilt*, in which a highly ritualized, though informal, quilting gathering becomes the vehicle as well as the metaphor for the intense personal narratives of the quilters. In addition to the focus on biographical stories, the occasion incorporates many other elements associated with women's ritualizing: the participants sit in a circle; the focus is on a domestic object; leadership and dominance fluctuate among the characters; women's skills are highlighted; whatever is of ultimate importance is realized through the relationships the group experiences and models; and so on.[9]

In rural settings, quilting rituals are often still the principal opportunity for women to ritualize together, and they are implicitly understood as such. Many quilts have religious significance, made in thanksgiving for some special blessing or healing or to honor the place of God in the quilter's life or to help raise money for a new church building. With purposes such as these in mind, the homely act of quilting becomes more than simply the production of a useful item and may represent a significant worshipful act. The Shakers, a religious group dominated by women, knew the truth of the relationship between spirituality and handmade goods; spurred by their motto "Hands to work, hearts to God," throughout the nineteenth century they produced domestic objects of particular grace, simplicity, and quality. Other activities from an earlier time include taffy pulls, autumn canning, and other rituals of food preparation that transcended their utilitarian culinary origins to become intimate, ritualized occasions for women to congregate, share stories and skills, and celebrate the essentials of women's life.

The countryside, however, has no monopoly on women's gatherings. In upscale urban drawing rooms and humble apartments, afternoon teas for women have also provided ritualized occasions for sharing, learning, and celebrating. That these events are more than just minor celebrations is evident from the ritual behaviors involved: unwritten rules for personal storytelling—and for stories about others, as well; the often regularly scheduled times and cycles of meeting; circular seating; meeting in women's homes; the focus on domestic experiences and skills, and so forth. Women's book and garden clubs provide opportunities for the same crucial functions.

An interesting example of women's ritualizing arose during World War II, when women, with husbands, sons, and fathers away, pitched in to aid the war effort by forming groups to roll bandages, write letters, and provide other kinds of support. Again, although the primary purpose of such ad hoc groups was utilitarian, I suggest that they were also subject to a natural tendency to ritualize. Just as the men (and the few military women) were able to ritualize their patriotism, defense instincts, and fear through donning uniforms, drilling, and learning new technology, volunteer women also ritualized their responses to the war, forming themselves into well-organized but often informal, leaderless groups that accomplished a stated practical purpose while simultaneously satisfying their need to participate in something of ultimate significance. Newsreels and other reports from the period dramatize these groups as meeting, proceeding, and understanding themselves in familiar, ritualized patterns.

Bridal and baby showers, too, are more than just parties, more than gift-giving occasions. They are the rituals of passage into marriage and motherhood in Western society, life events that are ritualized variously in cultures throughout the world. Once again, familiar elements recur: natural themes, domestic activities, circular arrangement, biographical narrative, respectful recognition of bodily processes.

These few examples provide evidence that the patterns characterizing women's ritualizing extend, not surprisingly, beyond specifically religious gatherings. This could, of course, also be said of men's activities—sporting events, clubs, conventions, military associations, and such; a case could be made that the hierarchical images and style of patriarchally developed religion apply in secular contexts as well. Moreover, there is no reason to suspect that women ritualize any more frequently or with any greater intensity than do men or mixed-gender groups.

Women's Ritualizing: A Distinctive Category?

What we can say with some confidence is that when women gather for ritualized occasions, they tend to behave in markedly distinctive ways.

Do Women Have a Distinctive Myth?

Lawrence Hoffman claims that "one of the prime functions of liturgy is the presentation of sacred myths to sacred assemblies."[10] Can women do this? Is there an underlying women's myth? For many worshiping women, the core myth remains that of their original faith group. Jewish and Christian feminists, for example, for the most part still adhere to the biblical account of the relationship of divinity and humanity—with an understanding that its poetic expressions are both metaphoric and incomplete. Other groups are developing mythical structures built on such concepts as the goddess, the earth, or the history of witchcraft. Still others represent the fruits of direct revelation, often as a variant on a dominant religion, as in the case of the Christian Scientists or Shakers.

Despite the prevalence of traditional myths in women's ritualizing, something akin to a common women's myth may also be emerging. Although its specifics may vary from culture to culture, its central elements seem to include a concern for preserving women's history, a reclamation of the connection of women with nature, respect and gratitude for the bounty of the earth, an emphasis on the stages of women's lives (maiden, mother, crone), and a celebration of women's reproductive and nurturing power. Female heroes who have made significant contributions to women's history provide legendary material woven into this myth-in-progress, as do recent reconceptualizations of the goddess. Still, it can probably not be claimed that at present a fully formed women's myth exists, though constitutive pieces of one appear to be swirling about, trying to coalesce.

Because it is difficult to imagine ritual without a corresponding stable myth—the traditional vehicle of the study of ritual—the absence of a stable myth in women's ritualizing could jeopardize its validity. However, the purpose and use of ritual in women's lives may suggest an alternative interpretation. In a religious and social system dependent on transcendent reality, myth assumes a crucial role; without it, there is no way to rationalize the inexplicable, no way to bring the transcendent into cognition. In such a system, myth and ritual work together to bridge a perceived gap between sacred and profane.

However, women are no longer able to relate to an image of the sacred that is transcendent, unearthly, and dominant, and have adopted instead an immanent understanding of divinity; they have little need of a narrative to explicate the nature of the holy. For such persons, the goal of ritualizing is less the expression and propagation of a foundational myth than the transformation of community. As Hoffman notes, the power of the myth lies not in its accuracy, but in its ability to "galvanize group identity."[11] Here again, performance theory suggests that the crucial element of ritual is what is *done*, not what is said or read. The lack of a fully developed women's myth, then, does not necessarily imply that women's ritualizing fails as a discrete category susceptible to analysis.

Sample Analytic Applications

If women's ritualizing qualifies as a definable area of study, it should yield distinctive insights in response to various analytic approaches. Two brief (and necessarily superficial) illustrations follow.

Women's Ritualizing as Ritual Criticism. In their almost relentless recontextualization of ritual elements both old and new, women in community have engaged, consciously or not, in an advanced form of ritual criticism, with resonance for academic ritual studies as well as for praxis.[12] This process has involved a variety of strategies.

The reflexivity built into women's ritualizing provides a mechanism for ongoing ritual criticism. By incorporating critical reflection as a necessary ritual element, women have ritualized critique—a process generally at home in academic conferences but unusual in worship settings. As we have seen and as Grimes remarks, "Ritual is a primary cultural means whereby participants learn to comprehend and criticize the constructedness of what are taken to be cultural facts."[13] Ritualizing women have utilized the constitutive quality of ritual to rewrite cultural assumptions and to alter the reality in which they live. By incorporating ritual criticism into the ritual itself, women have adumbrated the development of a subset of ritualization that is fluid and sensitive to time, place, and particularity.

Another manifestation of the effectiveness of ritualized self-critique is evident in the use of accepted scholarly critical methods to reveal

unexpected realities. Applying to traditional liturgical rites the herme-
neutic of suspicion learned from the biblical criticism of Schüssler
Fiorenza, for example, ritualizing women have revealed the covert—or
at least unarticulated—meanings that characterize rituals hostile to
women's well-being. The process has opened up possibilities for health-
ful and affirming ritualizing and has taught women the use of tools for
assessing ritual meaning, tools that can be applied to creative and redis-
covered elements as well as to traditional ritual forms.

As the meaning inherent in ritual acts and assumptions has been
revealed, women have been able to apply to ritual a kind of moral analysis more commonly understood as proper to ethics, an analysis particularly fruitful in uncovering both the manipulative strategies and failures
of justice submerged in traditional liturgies and the dominant ethnic
assumptions in newly developed rituals. Grimes suggests that a good
ritual genre incorporates its own critical mechanisms; this is clearly the
case with women's ritualization.

Women's Ritualizing as Feminist Analysis. Mary Margaret Fonow and
Judith Cook have outlined four themes that characterize feminist research and analysis: reflexivity, an action orientation, attention to affect, and use of the situation at hand.[14] Recognizing that these categories are neither exhaustive nor completely independent, Fonow and Cook
nonetheless suggest that any feminist analysis would incorporate and
reflect them. To the extent that women's ritualizing is coterminous with
feminist ritualizing—a common assumption in most of the extant literature, as we have seen, but one that needs careful deconstruction—it
should evidence these critical themes.

Under the general heading of reflexivity, Fonow and Cook identify
consciousness-raising and collaboration as examples of feminist methodology. Applied to women's ritualizing, these categories are exemplified in such elements as de-emphasis on formal leadership, egalitarian
planning styles, and the sharing of women's experience. More striking is
the direct reflection on the planning and execution of the ritual that is
so frequently a crucial part of the ritual itself. Reflexivity is manifest in
women's ritual imagery as well, with its focus on the circle—certainly
the most reflexive of all symbols.

A feminist action orientation, as understood by Fonow and Cook,
stresses political activity and the historical reconstruction of women's
struggles. In the ritual sphere, this surfaces in the conscious deployment
of various political strategies, the appropriation of the power to name,

and the reclamation of women's stories through personal narrative. This will to action is particularly pronounced, in a more literal way, in women's ritualizing. Although ritual, by its very nature, is an active endeavor, women have, to a large extent, rescued it from its entombment in texts and set it free to once more focus principally on activity. The most obvious evidence of this is the deliberate attempt to proliferate local and particular rituals that eschew permanent texts. In ritual imagery, this orientation is reflected in the honor accorded to such activities as craft making, mothering, and birthing. In ritual behavior, it is apparent in the stress on dance, on healing, on movement rather than stasis, and on vocalization rather than passive listening.

Attention to affect, for Fonow and Cook, means primarily attention to emotion. Women's ritualizing certainly attends to emotion—indeed, it fosters the open expression not only of such feelings as grief and joy, which can also be encountered at such traditional religious events as funerals, baptisms, bar and bat mitzvahs, and charismatic prayer meetings, but also of emotions that, with rare exceptions, would generally be unwelcome in religious settings—anger, sorrow, frivolity, assertiveness, playfulness. In this vein, the spontaneity and comfortableness of many women's rituals also evidence the prevalence of affective categories, as does the stress on memory and insight. Beyond the expression of emotion, the affective dimension might also include the emphasis on sensory experience that so often characterizes women's spirituality.

Finally, women's ritualizing clearly makes use of the situation at hand. The use of natural and domestic objects, actions, and skills falls into this category, as does the ad hoc creativity that produces ritual events. Celebrations of everyday life, of nature, and of the human body all contribute to a sense of the sacredness of the ordinary and available. Women's rituals are also commonly constructed around particular situations and needs in the life of the community. Whereas traditional rites tend to be nonthematic and generalized, women's ritualizing often focuses on issues—power, justice, or peace—or on individual needs brought by community members—healing from rape, the hope of conceiving, same-sex unions, thanks for the birth of a child, and so on.

Is Women's Ritualizing a Discrete Area of Study?

Before the question can be addressed of whether women's ritualizing is a discrete area of study, a prior issue must be considered, namely, what constitutes an area of study? What features would need to be present to establish the legitimacy of a distinct field of inquiry? Any list of such features would be somewhat arbitrary, but a number of rather obvious elements suggest themselves.

Distinctive Patterns and Practices. Women's ritualizing incorporates, as I have tried to demonstrate, a peculiar panoply of ritual patterns, images, and behaviors. In this regard, it clearly can be considered a recognizable field of its own. Although the features that characterize it are, for the most part, not unprecedented, their combination, use, and interpretation constitute a particular form of ritual expression.

A Definable Group of Practitioners. Although those communities of women that are actively engaged in their own ritualizing are not always easy to identify, and although many of them are comfortably involved not only in women's ritualizing but also in more conventional forms of worship, there clearly are large numbers of women ritualizing *as* women throughout the world. Of these, a significant proportion are intentionally committed to promoting women's ritualization as a valid, necessary, and meaningful alternative and/or supplement to mixed-gender worship.

A Discernible Developmental History. A discrete field should have a traceable course of development, convoluted though it might be; a movement that springs seemingly ex nihilo could lack depth, substance, and permanence. Women's ritualizing comprises a two-part historical development that includes both older, well-established religions and the more recent advent of feminist liturgy. This allows comparison with other ritual traditions as well as the promising application of newer scholarly insights.

Scholars and Literature. One obvious way a field of study is established is by becoming the object of scholarly attention. Women's spirituality has generated a large corpus of literature, both academic and popular; women's ritual behavior, as a subset of this larger topic, has increasingly been addressed in the literature, as the bibliography of this book indicates.

A Distinctive Methodology. Academic disciplines used to be identified largely by the particular methods they brought to analysis of the material at hand. More recently, such interdisciplinary fields as Latin American studies, religious studies, and international relations have demonstrated the advantages of combining a variety of methodological approaches in exploring the richness of a data set. Like these emerging disciplines, the study of women's ritualizing brings to bear a range of analytic methods.

A Reasonable Scope. To qualify as a legitimate field, an area of interest should probably have sufficient scope to address a meaningful segment of society and to provide insights that might reveal and benefit the larger society. Certainly women constitute a significant proportion of any society—more than half—but those who ritualize together are plainly a much smaller group. Nonetheless, the activities of that small group have ramifications that affect the society as a whole.

Significance. In the long run, the work of scholars and practitioners in a field should provide some useful information that helps us better understand ourselves and our environment and that advances the enterprise of learning. In this regard, the study of women's ritualizing has much to offer, expanding the scope of ritual studies, providing provocative insights into women's needs and behaviors, and opening avenues of inquiry previously thought to be closed or irrelevant.

Measured against the preceding criteria, women's ritualizing appears to be a legitimate and promising area of study.

Does Women's Ritualizing Constitute a New Ritual Genre?

Most of us, probably, were introduced to the term "genre" in connection with literature, where we learned it designated a particular type of writing—poetry, fiction, prose. Later, the concept became more nuanced as subgenres were introduced within these broader categories—biography, epic, sonnet, short story, and so on. It is never particularly clear where a literary genre ends and a simple form begins; this can only be deduced from the size and significance of the subject matter. The same difficulty applies, of course, to determining the boundaries of other fields of study.

Ritual studies is a developing interdisciplinary field largely defined by the work of Grimes since the 1980s. Although Grimes certainly has not been alone in establishing ritual studies, his early work in pulling together such seemingly disparate areas as liturgiology, drama, performance theory, and ethnography helped to consolidate the thought of far-ranging scholars who previously had not been in direct dialogue. In the last two decades, ritual studies has precipitated the publication of its own prestigious journal (*The Journal of Ritual Studies*), has established itself in the writings of a wide variety of investigators, and has become the subject of independent departments at numerous universities.

As with other disciplines, ritual studies almost immediately found itself classified into multiple subdivisions, as scholars staked out their interests and undertook the difficult task of bringing a fresh perspective to insights from related fields. Frederick Turner, tongue coyly in cheek, sees the process as a territorial exercise:

> At the edges of the worked area, heroic groundbreaking scholars hack out new fields from the wilderness. . . . When the work in one field becomes too difficult for the average trained researcher, the field splits into subfields, which may slowly attain the status of fields in themselves.[15]

This developmental process is clearly identifiable in ritual studies. Today, there are scholars in such subfields as area ritual studies (e.g., African ritual); subject studies (e.g., mythology and ritual); liturgics (religious ritual); and ritual cultural criticism, to name but a few.

Into this evolving milieu has been injected the exploration of women and ritual, largely through the work of feminist liturgiologists such as Procter-Smith. These scholars do not necessarily see their work as part of ritual studies per se, but it certainly has a place there. Their close identification with a particular discipline—in this case, liturgics— prompts the question of whether women's ritualizing is properly subsumed under that heading.

Although it is true that liturgical scholars and practitioners—Procter-Smith, Dianne Neu, Mary Collins, and so on—first mapped the field, it is equally true that liturgiology insufficiently covers the data. For one thing, liturgics explores the nature and praxis of worship; like theology, it presumes the commitment of the scholar to a particular ritual tradition. These early scholars generally have been Christians, searching for solutions to the problem of remaining self-aware women within the Christian dispensation. Likewise, most of the ritual reflections of Jewish, Afro-Caribbean, even Buddhist women are still firmly situated within established religions that the authors are reluctant to abandon fully. The situation is complicated by the feminist convictions of many of these scholars, which often lead them to commit themselves to reforming current religious organizations. This reinforces their institutional ties and necessarily limits their work to the somewhat narrower boundaries of liturgical studies.

Feminist theologians might also claim women's ritualization as part of their field. Rosemary Radford Ruether, Mary Daly, and other early Christian and Jewish theologians were the first to uncover the implications of women worshiping together and to suggest how that might be done and why. Their momentum has generally carried them beyond the question of ritual behavior, however; indeed, it has taken many of them beyond the bounds of theology, properly defined, at all. In any event, no one in this arena appears to be laying title to the study of women and ritual.

Anthropologists, who often consider ritual their exclusive turf, have also staked a plausible claim to women's ritualizing. Sered has broadened the field, as have ethnic chroniclers such as Karen McCarthy Brown, Virginia Kerns, and Marla Powers. Most of their work in women's ritualizing, however, has been rather peripheral to their larger interests in ethnography, generalized religious documentation, or cultural studies.

Thus, although women's ritualizing, like ritual studies itself, overlaps with and benefits from research in a variety of disciplines, it cannot be identified wholly with any one of them. This suggests that, if women's ritualizing can be considered a coherent area of study in itself, it (a) resides properly within ritual studies and (b) constitutes a prospective new subgenre of that discipline.

This, however, poses yet another complicating question: What is it to say that a field is "new"? This may seem a rather self-evident query at first glance, but the relationship of tradition, culture, and ritual brings into focus the question whether ritual behavior is ever "new" and whether whole new categories can be validly defined in studying it. Some would argue, with conviction, that although women may be ritualizing more these days (especially in intentionally feminist settings), this activity is insufficiently "traditional" to classify as an area of study in its own right. Moreover, I suspect that, among liturgiologists especially, there is a reluctance to accept the credentials of a movement generally understood to be marginal, political, and insignificant.

Eric Hobsbawm, among others, has addressed the question of the invention of tradition, considering the nature of both tradition and invention and the causal factors in the rise of new cultural behaviors. Hobsbawm contends that, rather than being static, tradition—which he defines, over against custom and routine, as a "set of practices, normally governed by overtly or tacitly accepted rules and of a ritual or symbolic nature"—can be and is frequently created anew.[16] Interestingly, Hobsbawm's discussion mentions factors in the development of traditions that mirror aspects of the growth of women's ritualizing. For example, he remarks that "objects or practices are liberated for full symbolic use when no longer fettered by practical use," calling to mind the incorporation of domestic artifacts into women's spirituality. He also comments on "the use of ancient materials to construct traditions of a novel type for quite novel purposes," suggesting that adapting older ritual practices into newer ones is a common factor of natural ritual evolution, rather than cultural raiding.[17]

Hobsbawm also outlines the social conditions under which new rituals develop:

> when a rapid transformation of society weakens or destroys the social patterns for which "old" traditions had been designed, producing new ones to which they were not applicable, or when such old traditions and their institutional carriers and promulgators no longer prove sufficiently adaptable and flexible.[18]

If Hobsbawm is concerned with the origin of new traditions, Bell comments in a similar vein on their consequences: "Ritual *can* be a strategic way to 'traditionalize,' that is, to construct a type of tradition, but in doing so it can also challenge and renegotiate the very basis of tradition to the point of upending much of what had been seen as fixed previously."[19] Clearly, these are precisely the conditions to which the development of women's ritualizing has responded.

Hobsbawm's work lays a foundation for considering the validity of newly emerging ritual patterns and for studying them with seriousness. Grimes goes further in describing and even advocating ritual creativity. Indeed, one of his "principles of ritualizing" is "the principle of ritual inventability: people can be taught to incubate ritual; traditions can be invented."[20] Grimes sees the emergence of new ritual patterns as a reflection of a world of pluralism and changing consciousness.[21]

If ritual patterns can and perhaps even should be invented afresh, then the newness of the most recent forms of women's ritualizing cannot disqualify them from consideration as significant ritual traditions. Nor can they be exempted from critical analysis. As Hoffman notes, in discussing the development of new methods in biblical research, it is crucial not only to bring to bear established forms of critique but also to utilize "approaches capable of constructing fields of meaning . . . congruent with contemporary criteria of meaningfulness."[22] The recognition of women's ritualizing as a distinct subgenre responds to this concern by assisting the larger cultural enterprise of discovering and redefining meaning in a postmodern world.

A last theoretical concern relates to the status and nature of genres themselves. Bell, for example (echoing Frederick Turner), complains with some justification that "categorization develops a dizzying momentum of its own."[23] Her critique derives not, as Turner's does, from a fear of academia run amok but from a concern with the issue of universals versus particulars that underlies much of current cultural criticism and that has influenced scholarship in most other fields of the humanities. Bell would agree with Michael Aune, who finds that "ritual and ritualizing are 'inherently historical' or radically contextualized with 'context' requiring as much interpretation as the ritual activities themselves."[24] This postmodern consciousness implies, as Grimes notes, "a dissolution of genres," in that each performance is perceived as unique, constituted by its own particulars, and detached from "traditional value systems and ideologies."[25]

Necessarily, there is a limit to the logical extension of postmodernist thought in this regard: it can suggest and even demand the annihilation of categorization, but only to the point that it finds itself with nothing left to talk about. Both thought and action are about relationships; although it is possible to discuss and enact the relationships among individual entities, the need to gather them into groups of like things is irresistible and even, perhaps, the crucial first step in developing the ability to converse at all. Ritual behavior, too, is quintessentially about relationships; if there is to be ritual study at all, it must use comparative methodologies.

It may be that postmodernism is on target and scholarly inquiry is riding the tail end of genre studies. It may not even be too outrageous to wonder about the ironic confluence of the end of an entrenched epistemic system just as women and other marginalized groups begin to establish themselves within it. Nonetheless, Grimes concludes that the postmodernist claim that we are beyond genres "goes too far—genres are always being made up and dissolving."[26] Bell acknowledges this tendency in her discussion of the postmodernist emphasis on performance theory, of which she notes that "its focus on ritual, theater, or sports as 'genres' or 'universals' of performance appears to involve the construction of very traditional types of relationships and categories."[27] Thus, perhaps, genres are with us to stay, and it may still be possible to talk meaningfully of women's ritualizing as a new subgenre within ritual studies.

But first, one final question must be posed: Is the study of women's ritualizing significant enough, substantial enough, and compelling enough to be considered a valid and viable subgenre at all? After all, as Grimes himself points out in discussing new ritual forms that might evolve into subgenres, some "are new, self-conscious, disestablished. Either they are small and therefore not important, or they are secondary because they are not enduring."[28] A critic could be excused for suggesting that either of these caveats might be applicable to the study of women as ritualizers. The evidence indicates, however, that women's ritualizing, whether quietly practiced over hundreds of years in dominant patriarchal cultures or developed anew as women find their own spiritual experiences and voices, is of extreme importance not only in the lives of individual women but also to the fuller understanding of ritual behavior.

Problems and Prospects

Although women's ritualizing is a growing phenomenon attracting significant scholarly attention, its permanence (not to mention growth) is far from ensured. Especially in its more contemporary forms, it faces numerous challenges, both theoretical and practical, that could marginalize or trivialize the movement or cause it to self-destruct.

The Postmodern Challenge

The Problem of the False Universal. The insights of postmodernist thought present critical challenges to the study of women's ritualizing. Chief among these, as we explored very briefly earlier, is the question of whether we can legitimately discuss generalized categories—even such seemingly self-evident and necessary classifications as "ritual" and "women." For some thinkers, "religion" itself is an empty construction of scholarship, a meaningless concept outside the particularities of individual practice.[29] Moreover, "there is little possibility of a shared, cross-cultural terminology that affords systemic methods of analyzing" religion.[30]

This dismal prospect, generally accepted, would toll the death knell for religious studies, including its various genres. Given these premises, women's ritualizing comprises no more than isolated ritual performances by particular women, with no valid commonalities arising from anything other than coincidence. The consequences of such a conclusion ripple outward, encompassing ever larger territory. Feminist scholars, for example, are wrestling with the problems inherent in the concept of "women's experience." Mary McClintock Fulkerson, among others, although denying the validity of the assumption of common experience, concludes that in a postmodernist reality in which experience is understood solely as particularized, "the basis for feminist theology—or any theology—as an academic discourse dissolves."[31] A dilemma arises especially for liberationists, who find it difficult to make their case if the oppressed, in general, and specific groups within that category cannot be identified in a way that can raise consciousness and provoke change.

Recently, religious studies scholars have been seeking an accommodation with postmodern thought while continuing to defend the legitimacy of comparative analysis. Wendy Doniger, Bell, and others are grappling with this negotiation. Bell, conceding much of the postmodern critique, nonetheless contends that most scholars recognize the limitations of their assumptions and terminology and of the attempt to know other cultures; thus, it is inappropriate "to conclude that we can know nothing, or that all attempts are politically, epistemologically, and morally suspect."[32] Still, postmodernism poses a conundrum for thematically unified cross-cultural studies, and its impact on the further investigation of ritual behavior among women and other collectivities remains to be seen.

The Failure to Acknowledge Difference. Closely related to the problem of universalizing is the concomitant inability to recognize adequately the differences among persons commonly thought to be alike. Jane Lewis notes that feminism has always had difficulty in "reconciling equality and difference."[33] Of late, feminist scholars have paid close attention to issues of race, class, and sexual preference—but of course, these, too, predicate generalizations. Jane Caputi suggests that feminism can still validly assume commonalities, at least in one regard: "Female bonding and myth-making can occur based not on some illusory all-embracing female culture, but on women's common 'Otherness' to patriarchy."[34] In contrast, Fulkerson broaches the awkward question whether, even though feminism carefully attends to oppressed women—*mujeristas*, Asians, lesbians, and so on—it is broad enough to embrace those women who are not feminist or are not even in sympathy with feminist thought.[35]

The rather ludicrous errors of some early anthropologists point to the dangers of ignoring the peculiarities of individual cultures; all too often, applying patterns observed in one tribe to a tribe in other circumstances resulted in stereotyping and fallacious conclusions. Moreover, says Margaret Mary Kelleher, discussing the work of Renato Rosaldo, assuming that culture is comprised of coherent patterns may lead a researcher to overlook "signs of change, inconsistencies, conflicts, and contradictions" that may be significant.[36] It is hardly debatable that geography, age, position within the dominant social structure, environment, and other specifics can and do influence the way that, for example, a culture ritualizes. The counterchallenge is to ask whether this fact precludes the correlation of any meaningful similarities that transcend cultural specifics.

In the case of women's ritualizing, practices vary widely from community to community, culture to culture, perhaps even from woman to woman; the many common elements that arise in some form virtually everywhere are not, therefore, insignificant. Beyond the details of time, place, and personality, there are surely some features of human existence—in this case, either sex-based biological data or gender-based experience—that arise whenever people form human community or seek spiritual expression.

The Loss of Meaning. With its emphasis on performance rather than referential meaning, postmodernism has called into question accepted assumptions about ritual. Grimes lists them:

(1) that its building blocks are symbols;

(2) that symbols are the carriers of meaning;

(3) that the meaning of a symbol is that to which it refers;

(4) that ritualists "believe in" these meanings.[37]

Citing the work of Dan Sperber, Grimes suggests that even the act of interpreting ritual symbols is simply the invention of more symbols, rather than a true explanation.[38]

Grimes's suspicion of "meaning" echoes a general postmodernist rejection of meaning as the goal of ritual. Granted this position, the creative adoption and active assignment of meaning to symbolic objects and actions that is at the core of women's ritualizing may represent an appeal to a false cultural norm. However, ritual theory also suggests that beyond the meaning accorded to the referents of a ritual's symbols (or instead of such meaning), there is also meaning in what a ritual does[39]— thus the increased attention to performance as the key to ritual value. In this regard, women's ritualizing has the opportunity to transcend earlier assumptions and to stress directly the meaning of doing, allowing meaning to arise from actions rather than being imposed on them, as Grimes says.[40]

Feminism and Ritualizing

For those ritualizing women who are consciously feminist, other potential difficulties arise from the nature of the movement itself.

Is the Movement Representative of All Women? As Fulkerson pointed out, intentionally feminist liturgies may not be hospitable to all women, especially to those who do not identify themselves with the movement. The vast majority of worshiping women continue to participate in the rituals of dominant religions, regardless of how patriarchal they may appear to others. Some critics question whether extremely liberal groups such as Women-church shut out relatively conservative women.[41] Although women of all ages and backgrounds continue to join in women's rituals, the question remains whether the movement can ever prove attractive to a substantial percentage of women.

Conversely, the mere "fact that women create or control an organization does not necessarily mean the organization will advocate female dominance or even gender equality."[42] Phyllis Schlafly, for instance, has formed groups of women to fight the Equal Rights Amendment and to advocate conservative roles for women.

A more complex problem under this general heading involves a kind of exclusive inclusiveness that extols the variety of practices that women bring to worship but extends this idea to an extreme that ultimately turns on itself. As Peter Steinfels reports in a 1993 *New York Times* article describing a Women-church conference, the commitment to include the rituals of women of varying ethnic and religious backgrounds backfired when the Native American contingent objected to the use of drums as a kind of ritual imperialism. As Steinfels argues, the silencing of the drums in an attempt at deeper inclusivity effectively "excluded those who found some value in incorporating an Indian ritual into their own celebration" and affirmed the right of the Native Americans to exclude. Despite its long reach across racial and cultural dividing lines, Steinfels continued, Women-church clearly drew alternative excluding lines in the sand.[43]

Internal Differences. Thought is hardly monolithic within the feminist community. As Carol Christ and Judith Plaskow remark, feminists hold very different views on such issues as "the nature of the alienation produced by sexism, the sources of liberating vision, and the future toward which feminism is striving."[44] Cynthia Eller notes that there two "centers of gravity" within feminism, which she denotes as "political" feminism and "cultural" feminism, the former concerned with confronting society and using the law as a remedy for sexism, the latter focused on creating a new culture built on inherently female qualities.[45] Within feminism, ideological and strategic differences arise as primary commitments and political agendas vary. Conflicts can result when theoretical and practical goals collide.

These tensions are present in studying how women do ritual. Bell comments that "ritualizing both implies and demonstrates a relatively unified corporate body, often leading participants to assume that there is more consensus than there actually is."[46] Ritual interpretation can also vary; David Kertzer remarks that problems may arise over "which symbolic understandings are appropriate: what roles should exist, what the 'issues' are, and which are worth fighting over."[47]

Small groups that coalesce around common concerns can fragment as they grow larger. Growth can also change the quality of ritual action; as Diane Stein notes, "It is impossible to ask each woman in a festival what her needs are," although such attention to the individual is highly valued in feminist ritual.[48] Again, "whereas broader social values might be identified by the group, the values of individual participants may not be shared widely."[49]

The Elusive Egalitarian Goal. Closely tied to these concerns is the difficulty of achieving truly nonhierarchical ritual organizations. Bruce Lincoln notes the "multitude of ways in which hierarchy may be reasserted, the most egalitarian of claims and intentions notwithstanding."[50] Unacknowledged but undeniable ritual skill, administrative talent, strong personality traits, and personal charisma all serve to stratify groups, no matter how committed they are to horizontal organizational models.

The Tension between Collectivity and Self. As articulated by Charlotte Caron, feminist ritual is intentionally collective and in clear contradistinction to "the New Age stress on individualism, personal well-being, and creation of one's own choices and realities."[51] The issue seems somewhat more complex than that, however. Grimes, conceding that "the usual scholarly argument is that ritual has little or nothing to do with the self and everything to do with the group," nonetheless notes that in the kind of "countercultural ritualizing" characteristic of women's worship, ritual functions "as a self-enhancing, self-enriching activity."[52] He suggests that this concern with self, however narcissistic, is allied with the emphasis on "experience" as a value.

These foci—concern for the individual, personal growth, and spiritual experience—are not found solely in "New Age" manifestations of women's ritualizing but are key values of women at worship in almost any setting, most certainly in feminist ritual. As Kay Turner says, for example, "For women, the ritual setting is often a place for naming individual powers and sharing the affirmation of those powers within

the group or simply internalizing them, through private ritual procedure."[53]

The egalitarian and collective aims of feminism are clearly in tension
with, but not necessarily in conflict with, the expressed importance of
the self. Grimes points out that the self itself is a cultural construction
and that "there is no such thing as an unsocialized individual, thus no
such thing as an asocial rite." "Too often," he continues, "individual
and group are construed as mere static opposites when in reality they
are dialectical pairs that presuppose and require one another."[54]

Community Cohesion. Community cohesion is a running issue in
women's spirituality groups, which often find it elusive and difficult to
maintain. Many women come to such groups primarily in rejection of
traditional patriarchal worship but not always with clarity and seldom
with unanimity on positive binding principles. This problem is exacer-
bated by the feminist preference for avoiding prescriptive and normative axioms and for advocating ecumenicity and inclusiveness. Groups
often find themselves with an ever-shifting membership, a phenomenon that has the advantage of providing a steady influx of "new blood"
but that places a premium on dwindling reserves of "old blood." Although some groups have happily achieved stability, the "censoring-in"
process is still far from complete in many others.

"Censoring out," on the other hand, as Lawrence Hoffman elaborates, defines what is unique about a group, what distinguishes it from
others. This is a tricky process. As Hoffman says, "We dare not be perceived as being precisely the same as others, but equally, we fear being
labeled as so different that we do not count."[55] Although many women
might renounce any competitive intentions in forming religious groups,
Hoffman posits that censoring out is both value-neutral and implicit in
all religious group formation. Indeed, while women's groups are unlikely to compete for members among themselves, distinguishing among
the many overlapping types of groups is problematic: the lines between
goddess religion and Wicca, for example, are impossible to draw, and
Christian feminism and Women-church often include many of the same
women. Women often associate with a particular group because they
know someone already in it; whether they will find themselves in agreement with the group's values, goals, and practices is difficult to predict.
The censoring-out process, too, then, contributes to a certain nomadism among women's spirituality communities.

As the women's ritual movement evolves, it—or at least individual
communities within it—will face the inevitable problems of developing

institutions: self-definition, codification (or not) of a common agenda, member identification, and burnout among the natural leaders. Feminist ritualizers, relying on their inherently egalitarian and ecumenical approach, hope to avoid some of these difficulties while fostering a new model of religious community building.

Weaknesses of the Leadership Model. Ideals of feminist ritual leadership include what Caron describes as "practices of shared leadership, rotating leadership, and having different people be responsible for different aspects." Caron concedes that leaderlessness is more problematic, but she identifies the goal as the limitation of hierarchy. Still, natural leaders do evolve, whether through force of personality or through skill. Caron cites Starhawk in noting the difficulties that arise when leadership is not recognized: leaders must pretend not to be influential, cannot be held accountable, and are unable to lead consistently. "Power is concealed and no one feels safe," Starhawk concedes.[56]

One feminist objection to solitary leadership involves resistance to institutionalization. It is generally assumed, Ann Braude notes, that women's leadership evolves most often when it appears to be authorized by direct spiritual revelation or experience rather than by institutional ordination. But this, she contends, usually applies only in the early development of a religious movement. Later, some form of institutionalization evolves to ensure the survival of the movement into subsequent generations. With that evolution inevitably comes institutional legitimation of authority. In religions founded by inspired women—Theosophy, for example, or Christian Science—the original authorizing vision of the founder was later replaced by organizational forms of leadership often exercised by men.[57] In some older religions, women's leadership is hereditary or authorized by social relationships and thus is preserved through the years. Feminist ritual communities will need to address the issue of leadership continuity in creative ways to survive the passage of time.

Problems of Ritual Practice

Temporality. New rituals are temporary rituals. The ad hoc quality of many women's rituals acknowledges this, as does the reluctance to perpetuate particular ritual forms by accumulating texts. In addition, comments John Hilary Martin, "creative rituals tend to lose popularity and die out after a time" as they are perceived to be isolated and discontinuous with the past.[58] Today's creative ritual insights can become passé very quickly; already, some of the rituals suggested by Ruether in 1985's *Women-Church* sound dated, and the exciting innovations of early women's worship have largely been left behind. The strength of women's ritualizing lies in its ability not only to innovate but also to combine and recombine old and new patterns to inspire new meanings and performances. Anachronistic practices need to be recognized and discarded, no matter how much nostalgia they may generate, and the worshiping community must be prepared to continue the creative process without the comfort of fixed texts and rubrics.

Coping with Ritual Failure. Grimes observes that although "participants probably experience the failure of ritual as often as they do the success of it," scholars generally ignore "rites that do not do what they are purported to do."[59] Ritualizing women encounter lots of failed ritual events, though they are often loath to admit it. Survival of the genre will depend in large part on the willingness of ritualizers to jettison ineffective ritual while refusing to become sentimental about it. The trick is to pass successfully from the period of experimentation to a phase in which ritual is more settled. Part of this process involves "learning how to engage in liturgy while remaining aware of its fictive, or, if you prefer, made up nature."[60]

Broadening the Symbology. Much of the imagery of women's ritualizing reflects a pastoral symbol set: natural landscapes (trees and plants, sun and moon, streams and seashores, dirt and rocks), country living (quilting bees, sunrise-to-sunset days, bread baking), and "old fashioned" approaches to women's realities (natural childbirth, cooking from scratch, herbal healing). It should thus be surprising, but somehow isn't, that most contemporary women's spirituality groups are found in cities. Are these symbols being claimed merely as a nostalgic reference to a more rural past? And although many of them are traditionally associated with women, do those associations still hold today?

Ritualizing women will, in time, need to incorporate symbols of urban life into their worship if they wish to add to their ranks those women for whom the city is the only environmental reality, particularly less socially privileged women. The symbols expressing women's spirituality must include metropolitan as well as bucolic images, references to poverty as well as to affluence, acknowledgment of technology as well as simplicity. Susan White notes that when we speak of human ritual subjects, we must take them "as we find them and not as we would wish them to be, and that it is unlikely that we can strip away the layers of civilization and modernity."[61] The same holds true for the setting, environment, ethos, and symbolization of ritual.

Risks for Ritualizing Women

Ghettoization. For many women, the development of rituals for women poses the risk of further isolation and the loss of meaningful interaction with the rest of the believing community. Procter-Smith is straightforward about the dangers: "The obvious risks are of being misunderstood and misinterpreted, of being attacked for heresy, of being further marginalized by those who desire to protect the status quo, of being rejected or dismissed as irrelevant."[62] Theresa Berger also addresses this concern, asking, "Does not this inculturation of the liturgy in the newly emerging 'women's culture' ultimately result only in a new 'ghetto-liturgy' for a previously marginalized segment of society?" Her response is that the goal of this process is to create a form of worship that is not exclusively the province of women but that—unlike current dominant religious rituals—includes women fully. Further, she contends, women's rituals serve "as a sign of the reshaping of liturgical life as a whole."[63]

Others might not react with such concern for the larger circle of believers. For Kay Turner, for example, separation is necessary and valuable, establishing through ritual the bonds that women use to generate social change.[64] Still others advocate the premise that women can and should create spiritual practices that are unique to them and that draw on their own strengths, avoiding the distortions of patriarchy altogether and contributing to the construction of more just societies.

The Failure of Community. Should women's ritualizing fail to produce some spiritually satisfying form of community, it could hardly survive. Certainly, the potential for self-delusion lurks in the creation of any worshiping community. Internal dissension can undermine both the perceived sense of unity and the legitimacy of the rituals. This risk is underscored by Bell's observation that "in most cases the community so constituted really does not quite exist outside the ritual."[65] This is certainly true for almost any worshiping group, which usually only assembles at a preset time for the ritual event itself; but in the case of ritualizing women, there may be other connections that shore up the sense of community—shared political beliefs, the word-of-mouth chain of relationships that brought the group together in the first place, common biological experiences, friendships, and so on.

Finally, Bell suggests that ritualizing groups are insecure because "ritualization leads participants to mistake the group's reformulation of itself as a straightforward communication and performance of its most traditional values."[66] This phenomenon, she suggests, makes ritualizing communities hothouses for the construction of power relations and limits their social efficacy.

To Resign or to Reform? At its inception, the women's ritualizing movement aimed principally to offer believing women an alternative locus for exploring their spirituality. Although some early members were unchurched, the larger percentage still maintained ties with their previous religion. This is not an uncommon model for women's religions; in some older cultures that include female-dominated religions, connections with the official or male-dominated religion of the region usually remain intact, and women may participate in both.

S. R. Skees, interviewing Women-church members, found that many still consider themselves Roman Catholics and still feel that the church is "home."[67] But, asks Ruether, is the goal of this continued participation to maintain nostalgic contact, or to reform patriarchal practice?[68] Ruether describes an ecumenical liturgy that included both Christian and pagan elements; this tendency toward eclecticism, she notes, is found not only in North American and Western European feminist circles but in Asia, Africa, and Latin America as well. For Third World women, the pre-Christian aspects of these rituals—foreign and ancient to most Western women—are often part of religions that remain alive in segments of their cultures. Ruether concludes that

> Women-Church has not made a decision to be either confined to Christianity or to move out of Christianity completely. It finds some Christian symbols reclaimable for feminism and others unredeemable. It is engaged in creating a new synthesis between the symbols it finds good in Christianity and symbols drawn from goddess religions. Its genius may lie in refusing to be forced into one side or the other.[69]

This accommodation may, against all odds, remain viable. Still, if sides must be chosen, it seems likely that most women in this situation will leave their traditional practices behind. As Skees quotes one participant, "It's more important to *be* church than it is to reform church."[70]

What Do Women Believe? This difficult question cannot be avoided in studying women's ritualizing. All too often, it is not entirely clear what exactly is being ritualized. Even if we grant the sort of immanent conception of deity that is common in women's gatherings, is (as Berger asks) "woman being celebrated rather than God?"[71] "God," of course, is a term that is not comfortable for many worshiping women—Schüssler Fiorenza has adopted the sign "G*d" in her writings to indicate the essential indescribability of deity—but Berger's inquiry can be expanded to include the varied understandings of the transcendent. Is a golden calf being erected in women's worship? Steinfels phrases the question differently, decrying "the movement's drift toward a kind of free-style Unitarianism, a creedless faith in an undefined divinity expressed in a profusion of rituals as well as in politically liberal good works."[72]

Without question, women's rituals celebrate womanhood, as both an inherent quality of the human condition and as a way of living. At the same time, the personal god of Western religion rings hollow as a conception of the ultimate. Both of these critiques assume that ritualizing must have a conventional object, a god, to be meaningful. This, for many worshiping women, may be a false assumption.

Imagination and Memory as Doable Acts

Richard Schechner has written that "the future of ritual is actually the future of the encounter between imagination and memory translated into doable acts of the body."[73] If, as Schechner predicted, this is where ritual is going, then women's ritualizing, despite the risks, may well survive and even thrive, for this is precisely what is enacted when women ritualize together.

In her first book, Procter-Smith titled a chapter "Something Missing: Memory and Imagination." For her, feminist ritualizing required a "reconstruction of our common liturgical memory" and an "enlargement of our common liturgical imagination," two deeply related though seemingly inimical categories.[74] Women's ritualizing is, at its core, about the recollection of a history that is lost in part and is present to women now only fragmentarily, mythologically, and symbolically. Its importance hinges not just on the stories that tell of heroic figures of the past but also on its evocation of that "great cloud of witnesses," the uncountable millions whose DNA women replicate, whose experiences women somehow share, whose labor pains and physical subordination and hopes and dreams women understand with great clarity. Women's ritualizing is largely about reclaiming and celebrating that dim memory.

But its dimness also requires an imaginative leap, a reconstructive effort that brings the memory into focus and projects it into the future. The power of imagination—to dream a world in which women are valued agents of their own material and spiritual lives—is understood by women to be an irreducible requirement of spirituality. The imaginative enterprise fills in the blanks, creates ritual actions of lament and celebration and healing, projects the possibility of genuine community, and posits a time of reconciliation and full personhood.[75]

The achievement of bridging memory and imagination is possible only through act, through the embodied performance of authentic human living. Ritual is a vehicle for that act and, even more, is the act itself. For women, acting is crucial, because both memory and imagination demand it and because the embodiment of women has so long been refused.

Women's ritualizing participates in what Schechner calls the "molten, creative core" of ritual that "demands that human life—social, individual, maybe even biological—keep changing."[76] Clearly, it must evolve if it is to be recognized as a new religious genre with a unique portfolio—the drawing together of persons with similar experiences of reality to explore spiritual truth in that context.

What distinguishes women's ritualizing from, say, the Metropolitan Community Church (MCC), which also gathers folk of like experience (gays and lesbians) for worship, is that whereas MCC reinforces and accesses traditional (Protestant Christian) ritual behavior in the interest of assimilation, women have used ritualizing to transcend tradition and to redefine social statuses. In part, this is attributable to the political dimension of women's ritualizing, but more important is the power of memory and imagination to reconstruct reality. The ritual process, in this case, opens up the prospect of a total redefinition of self, community, society, and sacredness.

To justify the proposal that it be considered a valid ritual subgenre, women's ritualizing must demonstrate not only the characteristics outlined here but also longevity. It must remain adaptive without becoming formless; it must build coalitions and either an institutional life or a viable substitute for one; it must coherently enhance spiritual awareness, not merely glorify the self or the group; it must generate meanings that can be of value to the human community as a whole. Were it to achieve this, it would truly be a revolutionary movement in the history of spiritual practice and a radical redefinition of religious ritual.

notes notes notes notes notes notes **notes** *notes notes*

Introduction

1. For more on this development, see, for example, Merlin Stone, *When God Was a Woman* (New York: Dorset, 1976).

2. Margaret Thompson Drewal, *Yoruba Ritual: Performers, Play, Agency* (Bloomington: Indiana University Press, 1992), 172.

3. A. P. Abbie, *The Original Australians* (New York: American Elsvier, 1969), 125; quoted in Nancy Auer Falk and Rita M. Gross, *Unspoken Worlds: Women's Religious Lives* (Belmont, Calif.: Wadsworth, 1989), 258.

4. Marjorie Procter-Smith, *Praying with Our Eyes Open* (Nashville: Abingdon, 1995), 19. Procter-Smith's principal concern is with Christian feminist prayer, but this list of caveats has cross-cultural applications.

5. The word "traditional" is used guardedly in this book to refer to established religions with deep cultural roots, as contrasted with forms of women's spirituality developed in the latter half of the twentieth century in the West. See Susan Starr Sered, *Priestess, Mother, Sacred Sister: Religions Dominated by Women* (New York: Oxford University Press, 1994).

6. Sered could perhaps have developed this aspect of her analysis further. She also lumps together all women's spirituality groups under the heading "feminist." In fact, many are not.

7. See Caroline Walker Bynum, "The Complexity of Symbols," in *Gender and Religion: On the Complexity of Symbols*, ed. Caroline Walker Bynum, Stevan Harrell, and Paula Richman (Boston: Beacon, 1986), 12.

8. Mary McClintock Fulkerson, *Changing the Subject: Women's Discourses and Feminist Theology* (Minneapolis: Fortress, 1994), 6, 8.

9. Esther D. Reed, "Whither Postmodernism and Feminist Theology?" *Feminist Theology*, no. 6 (May 1994): 17.

10. Denise J. J. Dijk, "Developments in Feminist Liturgy in the Netherlands," *Studia Liturgica* 25, no. 1 (1995): 124.

11. Marjorie Procter-Smith, "In the Line of the Female: Shakerism and Feminism," in *Women's Leadership in Marginal Religions: Explorations Outside the Mainstream,* ed. Catherine Wessinger (Urbana: University of Illinois Press, 1993), 36. Compare Procter-Smith, *Praying with Our Eyes Open,* 41–56.

12. See Carol P. Christ and Judith Plaskow, "Introduction: Womanspirit Rising," in *Womanspirit Rising: A Feminist Reader in Religion,* ed. Christ and Plaskow (San Francisco: HarperSanFrancisco, 1979), 7–9; and Plaskow and Christ, eds., *Weaving the Visions: Patterns in Feminist Spirituality* (San Francisco: HarperSan Francisco, 1989), 3–4.

13. Fulkerson cites the work of Tania Modleski, *Feminism without Women: Culture and Feminism in a "Postfeminist" Age* (New York: Routledge, 1991).

14. Falk and Gross, *Unspoken Worlds,* 57.

15. Bynum, "Complexity of Symbols," 13.

16. Fulkerson, *Changing the Subject,* 57.

17. Sered, *Priestess, Mother, Sacred Sister,* 8.

18. Ibid., 283.

19. Ibid., 11.

20. John Hilary Martin, "Introductory Essay," in *Religious and Social Ritual: Interdisciplinary Explorations,* ed. Michael B. Aune and Valerie DeMarinis (Albany: State University of New York Press, 1996), 19.

21. Rollo May, *The Cry for Myth* (New York: Norton, 1991); quoted in Gerard A. Pottebaum, *The Rites of People: Exploring the Ritual Character of Human Experience,* rev. ed. (Washington, D.C.: Pastoral Press, 1992), 43.

1. Defining Women's Ritualizing

1. See Sered, *Priestess, Mother, Sacred Sister;* and Wessinger, *Women's Leadership.* These groups include, among others, the New Thought movement, African American Spiritual churches in New Orleans, and Theosophy. The authors in this collection are generally less sanguine about the dominance of women in these sects than is Sered. Sered readily admits that her choice of religions is arbitrary (39–40). I question her inclusion, for example, of the Shakers and American Spiritualism, both of which were quickly dominated or manipulated by men after their founding by women; and other presentations of Korean kut ceremonies suggest that they are considerably less under the control of women than Sered suggests. It is also unfortunate that she chose not to discuss religions that have expired, some of which provide more convincing cases than those she examines.

2. See Charlotte Caron, *To Make and Make Again: Feminist Ritual Thealogy* (New York: Crossroad, 1993), 156–63.

3. See Cynthia Eller, "Twentieth-Century Women's Religion as Seen in the

Feminist Spirituality Movement," in Wessinger, *Women's Leadership*, 192. Eller suggests that Jewish women retain their Jewish identity after becoming feminists, unlike Christians, but she does not discuss them further.

4. Rosemary Radford Ruether, *Women-Church: Theology and Practice* (San Francisco: Harper & Row, 1985), 2. The term "women-church" originated with Elisabeth Schüssler Fiorenza.

5. Eller, "Women's Religion," 182.

6. Christ and Plaskow, "Introduction," 11.

7. Starhawk, *The Spiral Dance* (San Francisco: HarperSanFrancisco, 1979), 6.

8. See Caron, *To Make and Make Again*, 37–39; and Ronald L. Grimes, *Ritual Criticism: Case Studies in Its Practice, Essays on Its Theory* (Columbia: University of South Carolina Press, 1990), 110.

9. See Gillian Lindt Gollin, *Moravians in Two Worlds: A Study of Changing Communities* (New York: Columbia University Press, 1967), 74, 90. An obvious parallel exists here to accounts of convent life.

10. Valerie Saiving, "The Human Situation: A Feminine View," *Journal of Religion* 40 (April 1960): 100–112; Rosemary Lauer, "Women and the Church," *Commonweal* 79, no. 13 (20 December 1963): 365–68; Mary Daly, *The Church and the Second Sex: With the Feminist Postchristian Introduction and the New Archaic Afterwords* (Boston: Beacon, 1985).

11. Mary Daly, "Original Reintroduction," in *Beyond God the Father: Toward a Philosophy of Women's Liberation* (Boston: Beacon Press, 1985).

12. Daly, *Church and the Second Sex*, 11–14.

13. See Kay Turner, "Contemporary Feminist Rituals," in *The Politics of Women's Spirituality: Essays on the Rise of Spiritual Power within the Feminist Movement*, ed. Charlene Spretnak (New York: Doubleday, Anchor, 1982), 232.

14. Arlene Swidler, *Sister Celebrations* (Philadelphia: Fortress, 1974).

15. See Caron, *To Make and Make Again*, 2.

16. See Daly, *Gyn/Ecology*; and Eller, "Women's Religion," 174–78.

17. Patricia Malarcher, "Jubilee Ritual: A Creative Response," in *Women at Worship: Interpretations of North American Diversity*, ed. Marjorie Procter-Smith and Janet R. Walton (Louisville: Westminster/John Knox Press, 1993), 180.

18. See Anne R. Andersson, "Dismantling Patriarchy—A Redemptive Vision: Ritual and Feminist Critical Theology in Basic Ecclesial Communities," in *Women and Religious Ritual*, ed. Lesley A. Northup (Washington: Pastoral Press, 1993), 184.

19. Ruether, *Women-Church*, 7.

20. See ibid., 196–200.

21. Ibid., 57.

22. Ibid., 67.

23. Ibid. See also Mary E. Hunt, "Spiral Not Schism: Women-Church as Church," *Religion and Intellectual Life* 7, no. 1 (fall 1989): 82–92.

24. Dijk, "Feminist Liturgy in the Netherlands," 120–22.

25. See Bridget Rees, "Women Withdrawing," *The Way*, supp. 67 (spring 1990): 65–68. See also St. Hilda Community, *Women Included* (London: SPCK, 1991).

26. Mary Collins, "An Adventuresome Hypothesis: Women as Authors of Liturgical Change," in *Proceedings of the North American Academy of Liturgy* (1993), 48.

27. Marjorie Proctor-Smith, *In Her Own Rite: Constructing Feminist Liturgical Tradition* (Nashville: Abingdon, 1990), 20–35.

28. Marianne Ferguson, *Women and Religion* (Englewood Cliffs, N.J.: Prentice Hall, 1995), 174–89.

29. Theresa Berger, "The Women's Movement as a Liturgical Movement: A Form of Inculturation?" *Studia Liturgica* 20, no. 1 (July 1990): 55–64. In this book, the term "liturgy" is used in its plain sense, to mean worship or religious ritual.

30. Ronald L. Grimes, *Reading, Writing, and Ritualizing: Ritual in Fictive, Liturgical, and Public Places* (Washington, D.C.: Pastoral Press, 1993), 5.

31. Rebecca J. Slough, "'Let Every Tongue, by Art Refined, Mingle Its Softest Notes with Mine': An Exploration of Hymn-Singing Events and Dimensions of Knowing," in Aune and DeMarinis, *Religious and Social Ritual*, 188.

32. Rees, "Women Withdrawing," 66.

33. Susan Starr Sered, *Women as Religious Experts: The Religious Lives of Elderly Jewish Women in Jerusalem* (New York: Oxford University Press, 1992), 87.

34. Karen McCarthy Brown, *Mama Lola: A Vodou Priestess in Brooklyn* (Berkeley: University of California Press, 1991), 126.

35. See also Virginia Kerns, *Women and the Ancestors: Black Carib Kinship and Ritual* (Urbana: University of Illinois Press, 1989).

36. Marla N. Powers, *Oglala Women: Myth, Ritual, and Reality* (Chicago: University of Chicago Press, 1986), 196.

37. See Marigene Arnold, "Célibes, Mothers, and Church Cockroaches," in *Women in Ritual and Symbolic Roles*, ed. Judith Hoch-Smith and Anita Spring (New York: Plenum, 1978), 45–53.

38. Catherine Bell, *Ritual Theory, Ritual Practice* (New York: Oxford University Press, 1992), 109.

39. Tom F. Driver, *The Magic of Ritual: Our Need for Rites That Transform Our Lives and Our Communities* (San Francisco: HarperSanFrancisco, 1991), 31.

40. Bruce Lincoln, *Discourse and the Construction of Society: Comparative Studies of Myth, Ritual, and Classification* (New York: Oxford University Press, 1989), 119.

41. Grimes, *Ritual Criticism*, 19.

42. Sered, *Women as Religious Experts*, 126.

43. Grimes, *Ritual Criticism*, 119–20.

44. Ibid., 10.

45. Beverly Harrison, in the Mud Flower Collective, *God's Fierce Whimsy: Christian Feminism and Theological Education* (New York: Pilgrim, 1985), 113.

46. Sered, *Women as Religious Experts*, 6. This statement is arguably true for the anthropological study of all religions, as theology, not anthropology, has traditionally been the venue for discussions of belief. Moreover, the predicative aspects of a new movement generally attract more attention than do their more static objects. Sered defends women's role in a perceived dichotomy of men/ theology, women/ritual at some length (120–21).

47. Ruether, "The Women-Church Movement in Contemporary Christianity," in Wessinger, *Women's Leadership*, 207.

48. Starhawk, *The Spiral Dance*, 10.

49. Mary Farrell Bednarowski, "Widening the Banks of the Mainstream: Women Constructing Theologies," in Wessinger, *Women's Leadership*, 228–29.

50. See Robert Ellwood and Catherine Wessinger, "The Feminism of 'Universal Brotherhood': Women in the Theosophical Movement," in Wessinger, *Women's Leadership*, 75. Wessinger, in her introduction to the book, ponders the commonality of this theme in women's religions: "Does this emphasis reflect the age-old reliance of women on direct inner experience for religious empowerment? Or does women's outlook tend naturally to a concern with interconnectedness?" (14).

51. Sered makes the interesting observation that "polydeism characterizes almost all women's religions" (*Priestess, Mother, Sacred Sister*, 169). She acknowledges that she is broadly defining "deity" to include orishas, supernatural beings, saints, ancestors, and so on, but even with that panoply of possible deities, it seems hard to conclude that this is a universal phenomenon. Within feminist spirituality (one of her religions), for example, many women address a single Judeo-Christian god. Likewise, many pagans worship a single goddess. I suspect that whether women worship monotheistically or polydeistically has more to do with the larger traditions of their cultures than with beliefs distinctive to women.

52. Denise Dijk notes that recovery of the goddess is perhaps not widespread, commenting that "it is more common for American Christian feminists to speak of God or Goddess as woman-self, to equate God/dess with woman-self/Self" ("Feminist Liturgy in the Netherlands," 127).

53. Malarcher, "Jubilee Ritual," 189–90.

54. Margaret Farley, oral response to Lesley A. Northup, "Patterns in Women's Ritualizing," paper given at Yale University, November 1995.

55. See Barbara G. Myerhoff, "We Don't Wrap Herring in a Printed Page:

Fusions, Fictions, and Continuity in Secular Ritual," in *Secular Ritual: Forms and Meanings*, ed. Sally F. Moore and Myerhoff (Assen: Von Gorcum, 1977), 22. In her discussion of ad hoc rituals, Myerhoff notes that regardless of how improvisational they may be, they derive their elements from traditional rituals. Heather Murray Elkins (*Worshiping Women: Re-forming God's People for Praise* [Nashville: Abingdon, 1994]) asks some pertinent questions in this regard: "If a worship has been 'of service' to a community in a particular time, place, and social location, can it be transplanted? And if it can, should it be? Can one 'borrow' forms from racial, ethnic, and religion traditions other than one's own?" (141–42). She further notes that the answers are not clear but that Christianity (for example) is a "borrowing" religion and women are historically "borrowers." Sociologist Wade Clark Roof ("The Changing American Religious Landscape: Implications for Ritual," in *Proceedings of the North American Academy of Liturgy* [1994]) goes even further, saying that contemporary worship of all kinds represents an

> eclectic spirituality, borrowing images, myths, symbols, rituals and healing practices from such diverse sources as Asian religious traditions, Christianity, the occult traditions, nature religions, Native American and other native traditions, psychotherapy and the human potential movement. (25)

I would suggest that all religions are "borrowers." Nomadism, geographic expansion, conquest, cultural and mercantile exchange, religious seeking—all have brought different religious practices into contact. Seldom has this process left each religion "pure," and only the most isolated religions can make any claim to being unadulterated. Even then, most religious symbols, myths, and ritual techniques evidence startling commonalities across cultural boundaries, popping up in diverse places where contact cannot be demonstrated. A given culture would have difficulty demonstrating its unique ownership of any particular ritual element. Rather, ritual behaviors constitute a pool of archetypal resources from which various religions have dipped to find those that are most fitting to their own beliefs and practices. There are no property rights here. For example, as Karma Lekshe Tsomo, (in "Continuing the Conversation," in *Buddhism through American Women's Eyes*, ed. Tsomo [Ithaca, N.Y.: Snow Lion, 1995]), a Buddhist, notes, "Buddhism comprises a rich feast of cultural, intellectual, and spiritual traditions, from which Americans may borrow at will" (157). Nonetheless, the situation demands respectful sharing and sensitivity.

56. Collins, "Adventuresome Hypothesis," 46–47.

2. Emerging Patterns in Women's Ritualizing

1. These lists of ritual principles are general and are directed toward feminist liturgy. Still, when cross-referenced to each other, they fit closely with the

data shown here and provide a kind of graph of the relative importance of various elements. For example, commentators have stressed the relational nature of women's ritualizing and the need for shared leadership more than any other features. The embodied nature of women's worship and the need for it to be freeing for women have been the next most emphasized elements, followed respectively by inclusivity and respect for difference, the honoring of women's stories, an accent on daily life and experience, and the critiquing of patriarchy. A wide variety of desirable elements make up the remainder of the lists.

The lists consulted include those in Theresa Berger, "Women's Movement," 56–58; Caron, *To Make and Make Again*, 175–82; Mary Collins, "Principles of Feminist Liturgy," in Procter-Smith and Walton, *Women at Worship*, 12–15; Dijk, "Feminist Liturgy in the Netherlands," 126; June C. Goudey, "Worship and Gender: Toward Liturgies of Care," in *Proceedings of the North American Academy of Liturgy* (1993), 93; Rosemary Catalano Mitchell and Gail Anderson Ricciuti, *Birthings and Blessings: Liberating Worship Services for the Inclusive Church* (New York: Crossroad, 1992), 13–15; Dianne L. Neu, "Liturgical Life of Women-Church: Defining Our Terms," in *Women-Church Sourcebook*, ed. Neu and Mary E. Hunt (Washington, D.C.: WATERworks, 1993), 158–66; Marjorie Procter-Smith, "The Marks of Feminist Liturgy," in *Proceedings of the North American Academy of Liturgy* (1992), 69–75; Bridget Rees, "Women Withdrawing," 62; and St. Hilda Community, *Women Included*, 20–21.

2. David Kertzer, *Ritual, Politics, and Power* (New Haven: Yale University Press, 1988), 68.

3. Diane Stein, *Casting the Circle* (Freedom, Calif.: Crossing, 1990), 7.

4. Neu, "Planning Feminist Liturgy/Ritual," in Neu and Hunt, *Women-Church Sourcebook*, 19. Neu further considers naming the circle a critical element in women's ritualizing; she assumes the gathering of the women in a circle, with a litany or sharing of symbols that introduces the participants.

5. Michelle Levey, "Everyday Dharma," in Tsomo, *Buddhism through American Women's Eyes*, 65.

6. St. Hilda Community, *Women Included*, 22.

7. Rees, "Women Withdrawing," 69.

8. Carol Ochs (*Behind the Sex of God* [Boston: Beacon, 1977]), with other feminist thinkers, relates this emphasis to a distinctively female consciousness: "Both the earth and its cyclical nature are mirrored in the female menstrual cycle, hence the overwhelmingly feminine identification of cyclical time" (98).

9. This idea is discussed in greater depth in Lesley A. Northup, "Claiming Horizontal Space: Women's Religious Rituals," *Studia Liturgica* 25, no. 1 (1995): 86–102.

10. See Catherine Roach, "Loving Mother Earth: Some Reservations," *Hypatia* 6, no. 1 (spring 1991): 46–50. This article is also abridged in James E.

Huchingson, *Religion and the Natural Sciences: The Range of Engagement* (Fort Worth, Tex.: Harcourt Brace Jovanovich, 1993), 396–99.

11. Kay Turner, "Contemporary Feminist Rituals," 229. See also Catherine Bell, "The Ritual Body and the Dynamics of Ritual Power," *Journal of Ritual Studies* 4, no. 3 (summer 1990): 299–305.

12. Procter-Smith, *In Her Own Rite*, 52. Interestingly, Sered comes to the opposite conclusion in her study of women-dominated religions, claiming flatly that "women's religions do not seem to pay very much attention to women's bodies in any context" (139). This observation may perhaps reflect Sered's somewhat idiosyncratic choice of religions, many of which (Christian and East Asian sects, for example) have blossomed in cultures that otherwise diminish the role of the body or set it against the spiritual. Later in her book, however, she revises this claim, saying that "women's religions relate to bodies in distinctive ways" and noting that some honor women's bodies and that none consider them polluting (*Priestess, Mother, Sacred Sister*, 201).

13. Ruether, *Women-Church*, 111, 162, 200.

14. Sered, *Priestess, Mother, Sacred Sister*, 72.

15. Mitchell and Ricciuti, *Birthings and Blessings*.

16. Sered, *Priestess, Mother, Sacred Sister*, 139. Sered posits that women's religions, lacking the blood taboos of male-dominated worship, de-emphasize such matters as disposing of the afterbirth and becoming ritually clean after childbirth, acts typically ritualized in other religions. She also suggests (140), following Starhawk, that childbirth itself is so awesome that it hardly needs ritual elaboration.

17. Caron, *To Make and Make Again*, 137.

18. Sered, *Priestess, Mother, Sacred Sister*, 17, 145.

19. Sered, *Women as Religious Experts*, 89.

20. Colleen McDannell, *The Christian Home in Victorian America, 1840–1900* (Bloomington: Indiana University Press, 1986), 75.

21. Susan Wadley, "Hindu Women's Family and Household Rites in a North Indian Village," in Falk and Gross, *Unspoken Worlds*, 73.

22. Barbara Walker, *Women's Rituals* (San Francisco: HarperSanFrancisco, 1990), 45–49.

23. Dianne L. Neu, "Women Revisioning Religious Rituals," in Northup, *Women and Religious Ritual*, 155. Neu's article extensively uses the metaphor of weaving sisterhood.

24. Procter-Smith, *Praying with Our Eyes Open*, 67.

25. Caron, *To Make and Make Again*, 222.

26. Sered, *Priestess, Mother, Sacred Sister*, 198.

27. Susan Middleton-Keirn, "Convivial Sisterhood: Spirit Mediumship and Client-Core Network among Black South African Women," in Hoch-Smith and Spring, *Women in Ritual*, 202.

28. Collins, "Principles of Feminist Liturgy," 12.

29. Starhawk, *Truth or Dare* (New York: Harper & Row, 1987), 23.

30. McDannell, *The Christian Home,* 127.

31. Maria Harris, *Dance of the Spirit: The Seven Steps of Women's Spirituality* (New York: Bantam, 1989), 131.

32. Elisabeth Schüssler Fiorenza, "Emerging Issues in Feminist Biblical Interpretation," in *Christian Feminism: Visions of a New Humanity,* ed. Judith L. Weidman (San Francisco: Harper & Row, 1984), 51. The expanded version of this article is *In Memory of Her: A Feminist Reconstruction of Christian Origins* (New York: Crossroad, 1984).

33. Schüssler Fiorenza, "Emerging Issues," 51.

34. Ibid., 31.

35. See David C. Estes, "Ritual Validations of Clergywomen's Authority in the African American Spiritual churches of New Orleans," in Wessinger, *Women's Leadership,* 151.

36. Brown, *Mama Lola,* 55.

37. Melva Wilson Costen, "African-American Women and Religious Ritual," in Northup, *Women and Religious Ritual,* 16.

38. See Sered, *Priestess, Mother, Sacred Sister,* 5. Sered makes the valid point that these founders generally sacrificed authority as their religions became institutionalized—that is, as their shamanistic character became eclipsed by a more priestly model of spiritual leadership.

39. Walker, *Women's Rituals,* v–vi.

40. Starhawk, *The Spiral Dance* (San Francisco: HarperSanFrancisco, 1979), 40.

41. McDannell, *The Christian Home,* 93.

42. See Sered, *Priestess, Mother, Sacred Sister,* 60, 125.

43. Dianne L. Neu, "Celebrating Women's Power," *WATERwheel* 6, no. 4 (winter 1993–94): 4–5.

44. Riv-Ellen Prell-Foldes, "Coming of Age in Kelton: The Constraints on Gender Symbolism in Jewish Ritual," in Hoch-Smith and Spring, *Women in Ritual and Symbolic Roles,* 87.

45. See Malarcher, "Jubilee Ritual," 180.

46. Sue Seid-Martin, "Rituals for Re-Imagining," *Theological Markings* 2, no. 2 (summer 1994): 19.

47. Grimes, *Ritual Criticism,* 26, 166.

48. Elkins, *Worshiping Women,* 26–27.

49. Dianne L. Neu, "Examples and Ideas for Creating Feminist Rituals," in Neu and Hunt, *Women-Church Sourcebook,* 22–23.

50. Ruether, *Women-Church,* 110, 129.

51. Casey Miller and Kate Swift, *Words and Women: New Language in New Times,* rev. ed. (New York: HarperCollins, 1991), 88.

52. Sered, *Priestess, Mother, Sacred Sister,* 93.

53. Hoch-Smith and Spring, *Women in Ritual*, 20. For a brief historical background, see Lizette Larson-Miller, "Women and the Anointing of the Sick," *Coptic Church Review* 12, no. 2 (summer 1991): 37.

54. Chellis Glendinning, "The Healing Powers of Women," in Spretnak, *Politics of Women's Spirituality*, 285.

55. Neu, "Liturgical Life of Women-Church," 16.

56. Yvonne Rand, "Abortion: A Respectful Meeting Ground," in Tsomo, *Buddhism through American Women's Eyes*, 86.

57. Sered, *Priestess, Mother, Sacred Sister*, 6.

58. Stein, *Casting the Circle*, 58.

59. Walker, *Women's Rituals*, 167–73.

60. Stein, *Casting the Circle*, 49.

61. St. Hilda Community, *Women Included*, 22, 32.

62. Inez Adams, quoted in Estes, "Ritual Validations of Clergywomen's Authority," 152.

63. Procter-Smith, *Praying with Our Eyes Open*, 38.

64. See Sered, *Priestess, Mother, Sacred Sister*, 141.

65. See Estes, "Ritual Validations of Clergywomen's Authority," 157.

66. See Sered, *Priestess, Mother, Sacred Sister*, 225.

67. See Irene Monroe, "The Aché Sisters: Discovering the Power of the Erotic in Ritual," in Procter-Smith and Walton, *Women at Worship*, 132.

68. See Wendy Hunter Roberts, "In Her Name: Toward a Feminist Thealogy of Pagan Ritual," in Procter-Smith and Walton, *Women at Worship*, 145.

69. See Sered, *Priestess, Mother, Sacred Sister*, 37.

70. Anita Spring, cited in ibid., 60.

71. Sered, *Priestess, Mother, Sacred Sister*, 130–33.

72. Sara Maitland, *A Map of the New Country: Women and Christianity* (London: Routledge and Kegan Paul, 1983), 132.

73. Ruether, *Women-Church*, 171, 203.

74. Procter-Smith, *Praying with Our Eyes Open*, 66.

75. Sered, *Priestess, Mother, Sacred Sister*, 150.

76. Ibid., 133.

77. Ibid., 87.

78. See ibid., 134–37. Indeed, Procter-Smith (*Praying with Our Eyes Open*, 120) is led to question whether the eucharist is a suitable ritual meal even for Christian feminists, noting how seldom it is reconceived in feminist liturgies.

79. See Brown, *Mama Lola*, 65–66.

80. Kerns, *Women and the Ancestors*, 149.

81. Kay Turner and Suzanne Seriff, cited in Estes, "Ritual Validations of Clergywomen's Authority," 161.

82. See Sered, *Priestess, Mother, Sacred Sister*, 133.

83. Procter-Smith, *Praying with Our Eyes Open*, 134–35.

84. Ronald L. Grimes, *Beginnings in Ritual Studies* (Washington, D.C.: University Press of America, 1982), 50.
85. Prell-Foldes, "Coming of Age," 83.
86. Berger, "The Women's Movement," 56.
87. Rees, "Women Withdrawing," 66.
88. Eller, "Women's Religion," 181.
89. Kay Turner, "Contemporary Feminist Rituals," 228. This is an interesting comparison. While the shamanistic model is indeed valued in women's worship, the ritualist, even in feminist communities, seems more closely related to the role of priest than of shaman.
90. Wessinger, *Women's Leadership*, 13.
91. Kerns, *Women and the Ancestors*, 169, 176.
92. See Sered, *Priestess, Mother, Sacred Sister*, 80.
93. See ibid., 217.
94. Ibid., 78; *Women as Religious Experts*.
95. Stein, *Casting the Circle*, 86.
96. Ruether, *Women-Church*, 206–9.
97. Goudey, "Worship and Gender," 93. Mitchell and Ricciuto (*Birthings and Blessings*) emphasize instead the local, particular character of women's ritualizing, contrasting it with "most ecumenical or regional gatherings" (14). The authors seem to use the term "ecumenical" to mean an arbitrary grouping based on geography; I use it to designate egalitarian inclusivity.
98. Procter-Smith, *In Her Own Rite*, 21 (author's emphasis).
99. See Ruether, *Women-Church*; Walker, *Women's Rituals*; Mitchell and Ricciuti, *Birthings and Blessings*; and Neu and Hunt, *Women-Church Sourcebook*. *WATERwheel* is a periodical published by WATER in Washington, D.C. See also, for example, Shermie Schafer, "Return to the Dance: The Power of Ritual in 'Ordinary' Lives," in Northup, *Women and Religious Ritual*, 77–86; and Wendy Hunter Roberts, "In Her Name" (137–62) and Ada María Isasi-Díaz, "On the Birthing Stool: Mujerista Liturgy" (191–212), in Procter-Smith and Walton, *Women at Worship*.

Even though books such as *Birthings and Blessings* and those by Walker, Stein, and the WATER staff (including Neu and Hunt) are not scholarly works, they are invaluable sources of information about actual ritual practice. As with any feminist descriptive task, the line between formal scholarship and lived experience is deliberately and necessarily blurred. It remains to be seen whether such popularization will benefit or ossify women's ritualization, and whether the deemphasis on texts will remain an identifying feature of women's ritualizing.
100. See Henry Pernet, *Ritual Masks: Descriptions and Revelations* (Columbia: University of South Carolina Press, 1992), 136–49.
101. Sered, *Priestess, Mother, Sacred Sister*, 141. Sered also notes that in Okinawan women's religion, priestesses sometimes wear masks.

102. See Pernet, *Ritual Masks*, 152.

103. See Grimes, *Reading, Writing, and Ritualizing*, 107.

104. Kathryn Allen Rabuzzi, "Bodyworship: The Gender-Masquerade of Fashion, Beauty, and Style," in Northup, *Women and Religious Ritual*, 128.

105. Walker, *Women's Rituals*, 86.

106. Sered, *Priestess, Mother, Sacred Sister*, 138.

107. Grimes, *Reading, Writing, and Ritualizing*, 28.

108. Bynum, "Complexity of Symbols," 13.

109. Sered, *Priestess, Mother, Sacred Sister*, 130–33.

3. Ritualizing Space and Time

1. Mircea Eliade, *The Sacred and the Profane*, trans. Willard R. Trask (New York: Harcourt, Brace and Company, 1959).

2. Driver, *Magic of Ritual*, 57.

3. See Eliade, *Sacred and the Profane*.

4. See, for example, William Cenkner, review of *Mircea Eliade's Vision for a New Humanism*, by David Cave, *Worship* 68, no. 3 (May 1994): 267–68.

5. J. B. O'Connell, *Church Building and Furnishing: The Church's Way: A Study in Liturgical Law* (Notre Dame, Ind.: University of Notre Dame Press, 1955), 248.

6. Frédéric Debuyst, "The Church, a Dwelling Place of Faith," *Studia Liturgica* 24, no. 1 (1994): 43–44.

7. See Horst Schwebel, "Liturgical Space and Human Experience, Exemplified by the Issue of the 'Multi-Purpose' Church Building," *Studia Liturgica* 24, no. 1 (1994): 16–18.

8. On processions, see Grimes, *Reading, Writing, and Ritualizing*, 63.

9. Liviu Streza, "The Mystagogy of Sacred Space According to Orthodox Theology," *Studia Liturgica* 24, no. 1 (1994): 88.

10. At the 1993 Convention of the Association of Diocesan Liturgy and Music Commissions, Jackson, Miss.

11. See, for example, M. D. Chenu's *Nature, Man, and Society in the Twelfth Century*, (1957; reprint, Chicago: University of Chicago Press, 1968), which discusses the Pseudo-Dionysian thinking that saw "symbolic action [as] a normal part of the dynamism of a cosmos reaching upward toward God in hierarchical stages" (135).

12. Kay Turner, "Contemporary Feminist Rituals," 222.

13. Ronald L. Grimes, "Liturgical Supinity, Liturgical Erectitude: On the Embodiment of Ritual Authority," *Studia Liturgica* 23, no. 1 (1993): 39–60.

14. Ibid., 58.

15. Ibid., 40, 45, 52, 57.

16. George S. Worgul, *From Magic to Metaphor: A Validation of the Christian Sacraments* (New York: Paulist, 1980), 81. Worgul approvingly quotes B. R. Brinkman to the effect that "the upward looking seems to make the sacrament effective," whereas the backward look gives us hope that our "insufficient performance here and now" will one day be acceptable (81). This fiercely negative view of the horizontal dimension of ritual, with the concomitant assertion that "up" is good, unambiguously identifies the patriarchal vision of spatial reality.

17. Kath McPhillips, "Women-Church and the Reclamation of Sacredness," *Journal of Feminist Studies in Religion*, 10, no. 1 (spring 1994): 115–16.

18. Victoria Lee Erickson, "Victoria Lee Erickson Replies," *Journal of Feminist Studies in Religion* 10, no. 1 (spring 1994): 121. See also Victoria Lee Erickson, "Back to the Basics: Feminist Social Theory, Durkheim and Religion," *Journal of Feminist Studies in Religion* 8, no. 1 (spring 1992): 35–46; and *Where Silence Speaks: Feminism, Social Theory, and Religion* (Minneapolis: Fortress, 1993). On the exclusion of women from sacred space, see, for example, Barbara Borts, "Trespassing the Boundaries: A Reflection on Men, Women, and Jewish Space," in Northup, *Women and Religious Ritual*, 51–62.

19. Mary Daly, "Original Reintroduction," xxvii.

20. Edward T. Hall, *The Hidden Dimension* (Garden City, N.Y.: Doubleday, Anchor, 1969), 69, 181.

21. Sered, *Women as Religious Experts*, 51.

22. Eileen King, "A Lingering Question: What Is Feminist Prayer?" in Procter-Smith and Walton, *Women at Worship*, 225.

23. Collins, "Adventuresome Hypothesis," 46.

24. Roberts, "In Her Name," 140.

25. William Seth Adams, "An Apology for Variable Liturgical Space," *Worship* 61, no. 3 (May 1987): 241. Adams dismisses the first two objections as easily overcome, and suggests adaptations to mitigate the third.

26. James F. White, "Liturgy and the Language of Space," *Worship* 52, no. 1 (January 1978): 58.

27. Ruether, *Women-Church*, 150–51.

28. Dianne L. Neu, "Women Revisioning Religious Rituals," 155–72.

29. Mitchell and Ricciuti, *Birthings and Blessings*, 14.

30. Juan Eduardo Campo, *The Other Sides of Paradise: Explorations into the Religious Meanings of Domestic Space in Islam* (Columbia: University of South Carolina Press, 1991), 99.

31. Bynum, "Complexity of Symbols," 16.

32. Starhawk, "Ritual as Bonding, Action as Ritual," in Christ and Plaskow, *Womanspirit Rising*, 326.

33. Walker, *Women's Rituals*, 11.

34. Grimes, *Reading, Writing, and Ritualizing*, 65.

35. Proctor-Smith writes, "In gatherings of women, then, denominational, confessional, or traditional divisions are relativized" (*In Her Own Rite*, 25). I would contend that this relativizing process goes further, breaking down the division of sacred and secular as well. Along these lines, Kay Turner has related the concept of ritual activity to feminist networking, "a horizontal, earth-bound spreading-out and crossing of boundaries that insures the life-flow of relationship between structurally opposed social domains" ("The Virgin of Sorrows Procession: Mothers, Movement, and Transformation," *Arche: Notes and Papers on Archaic Studies* 6 (1981): 79).

36. Such a movement between women's ritualization and the wider secular culture is bitterly contested by traditional religious institutions, which are anxious to turn away evidences of creeping secular humanism such as women's reproductive rights or the separation of church and state. Liturgists, too, guard the sacred precincts: one of Aidan Kavanagh's pithy laws of liturgical style is "Adapt culture to the liturgy rather than liturgy to culture" (*Elements of Rite: A Handbook of Liturgical Style* [New York: Pueblo, 1982], 103).

37. See Neu, "Celebrating Women's Power," 4–5.

38. Bell, *Ritual Theory, Ritual Practice*, 141.

39. Grimes, *Reading, Writing, and Ritualizing*, 49.

40. Rees, "Women Withdrawing," 70.

41. Procter-Smith, *Praying with Our Eyes Open*, 57.

42. Catherine Vincie, "Gender Analysis and Christian Initiation," *Worship* 69, no. 6 (November 1995): 517.

43. Grimes, *Reading, Writing, and Ritualizing*, 72.

44. Catherine Vincie, "Rethinking Initiation Rituals: Do Women and Men Do It the Same Way?" in *Proceedings of the North American Academy of Liturgy* (1995), 161.

45. Grimes, *Reading, Writing, and Ritualizing*, 57.

46. Mary O'Brien, "Periods," in *Taking Our Time: Feminist Perspectives on Temporality*, ed. Frieda Johles Forman with Caoran Sowton, Athene Series (Elmsford, N.Y.: Pergamon, 1989), 14.

47. Elizabeth Deeds Ermarth, "The Solitude of Women and Social Time," in Forman, *Taking Our Time*, 41.

48. Prell-Foldes, "Coming of Age," 91.

49. O'Brien, "Periods," 16. Robbie Pfeuffer Kahn ("Women and Time in Childbirth and during Lactation," in Forman, *Taking Our Time*, 20–36) is more sanguine about Eliadean mythic time, by which she means a "return to origins," contending that it is directly related to pregnancy and childbirth: "Mythic time can be entered over and over, although its most intense expression, the formative expression, may come at the moment of birth" (27). Kahn shares little of Forman's concern about overidentification with nature (see quote

following), stressing the resonance of the rhythms of agricultural time with women's biological processes.

50. Heide Göttner-Abendroth, "Urania—Time and Space of the Stars: The Macrocosmal Cosmos through the Lens of Modern Physics," in Forman, *Taking Our Time*, 111.

51. Indeed, a magazine produced by and for girls, *New Moon*, plays on the theme not only in its title but also in its mascot personality, Luna.

52. Forman, *Taking Our Time*, 8.

53. Ibid., xiv.

54. Irma Garcia, "Femalear Explorations: Temporality in Women's Writing," in ibid., 167.

55. Ibid., 166.

56. Mary Daly with Jane Caputi, *Webster's First New Intergalactic Wickedary of the English Language* (San Francisco: HarperSanFrancisco, 1987), 98.

57. Daly, *Church and the Second Sex*, xvii–xviii.

4. Narrative and Women's Ritualizing

1. For Native American cultures, see Arvind Sharma, ed., *Religion and Women* (Albany: State University of New York Press, 1994), 42; for Korean, see Youngsook Kim Harvey, "Possession Sickness and Women Shamans in Korea," in Falk and Gross, *Unspoken Worlds*, 38; for Indian, see Doranne Jacobson, "Golden Handprints and Red-Painted Feet: Hindu Childbirth Rituals in Central India," in Falk and Gross, *Unspoken Worlds*, 65; for Moroccan, see Fatima Mernissi, "Women, Saints, and Sanctuaries in Morocco," in Falk and Gross, *Unspoken Worlds*, 113; and for Kurdish, see Sered, *Priestess, Mother, Sacred Sister*, 128.

2. Ruether, *Women-Church*; Walker, *Women's Rituals*, 125–30.

3. Caron, *To Make and Make Again*, 7.

4. Neu, "Women Revisioning Religious Rituals," 156.

5. Sered, *Priestess, Mother, Sacred Sister*, 220.

6. Elaine Lawless, "Not So Different a Story after All: Pentecostal Women in the Pulpit," in Wessinger, *Women's Leadership*, 42–43.

7. See David C. Estes, "Ritual Validations of Clergywomen's Authority," 161–64.

8. Fulkerson, *Changing the Subject*, 272–73.

9. Roof, "Changing American Religious Landscape," 25.

10. Fulkerson, *Changing the Subject*, 12.

11. James B. Wiggins, ed., *Religion as Story* (Lanham, Md.: University Press of America, 1975), 20.

12. William G. Doty, "The Stories of Our Times," in ibid., 115.

13. Wiggins, *Religion as Story*, 20.

14. Michael Novak, "'Story' and Experience," in ibid., 175.

15. As Fulkerson notes,

A narrative is in some sense the woman's account of herself, but it is also inscribed with other meanings, from being framed by its lodging in a mode of communication . . . to its prior inscription by the expectation of the interviewee of what the interviewer wants to know. (*Changing the Subject,* 380)

16. Regarding such deeper layers of engagement and response, see Stephen Crites, "Angels We Have Heard," in Wiggins, *Religion as Story,* 25.

17. For a somewhat fuller discussion, see Procter-Smith, *Praying with Our Eyes Open,* 58–59.

18. Ibid., 59.

19. *Ruach* 13, no. 2 (spring 1992): 8.

20. Catherine Bell, "The Authority of Ritual Experts," *Studia Liturgica* 23, no. 1 (1993): 108.

21. Aidan Kavanagh, "Textuality and Deritualization: The Case of Western Liturgical Usage," *Studia Liturgica* 23, no. 1 (1993): 77.

22. Sered, *Priestess, Mother, Sacred Sister,* 251.

23. Fulkerson, *Changing the Subject,* 49.

24. Arthur M. Schlesinger, introduction to *Pioneer Women: Voices from the Kansas Frontier* (New York: Simon and Schuster, Touchstone, 1981), 11.

25. Jane Lewis, "Women's History, Gender History, and Feminist Politics," in *The Knowledge Explosion: Generations of Feminist Scholarship,* ed. Cheris Kramarae and Dale Spender (New York: Teachers College Press, 1992), 158.

26. Angela McRobbie, "Dance and Social Fantasy," in *Gender and Generation,* ed. McRobbie and Mica Nava (London: Macmillan, 1984), 157.

27. Phyllis H. Kaminski, "Claiming Our Voices: A Teaching/Learning Experiment," *Journal of Feminist Studies in Religion* 10, no. 1 (spring 1994): 131.

28. Kathleen M. Dugan, "In the Beginning Was Woman: Women in Native American Religious Traditions," in Sharma, *Religion and Women,* 42.

29. Schüssler Fiorenza, *In Memory of Her,* 29.

30. Procter-Smith, *In Her Own Rite,* 48.

31. Sue Levi Elwell, "Reclaiming Jewish Women's Oral Tradition? An Analysis of Rosh Hodesh," in Procter-Smith and Walton, *Women at Worship,* 112.

32. Elizabeth Ozorak, "The Social Construction of Women's Religious Self" (paper presented at the annual meeting of the American Psychological Association, Toronto, August 1996).

33. Marjorie Procter-Smith, "Liturgical Anamnesis," *Worship* 61, no. 5 (September 1987): 420–21.

34. Reed, "Whither Postmodernism and Feminist Theology?" 24.

35. Linda Sexson, "Let Talking Snakes Lie: Sacrificing Stories," in *Paths to the Power of Myth,* ed. Daniel C. Noel (New York: Crossroad, 1994), 150.

36. See Grimes, *Ritual Criticism*, 166.

37. Wiggins, *Religion as Story*, 17.

38. Flora A. Keshgegian, "Scripting the Self/Subjecting the Transcendent: Autobiography and Feminist Theology" (paper presented at the annual meeting of the American Academy of Religion, Chicago, Ill., 1994).

39. Diane Purkiss, "Women's Rewriting of Myth," in *The Feminist Companion to Mythology*, ed. Carolyne Larrington (London: Pandora, 1992), 451.

40. Sexson, "Let Talking Snakes Lie," 144.

41. Caron, *To Make and Make Again*, 74.

42. Mary Grey, "Method in Feminist Theology," *Feminist Theology*, no. 6 (May 1994): 99.

43. Grimes, *Ritual Criticism*, 166.

44. Ibid., 158.

45. Ibid., 166–67.

46. Ibid., 162.

47. Marsha Aileen Hewitt, *Critical Theory of Religion: A Feminist Analysis* (Minneapolis: Fortress, 1995), 110.

48. Grimes, *Reading, Writing, and Ritualizing*, 9, 24.

49. Grimes, *Ritual Criticism*, 171.

50. Caron, *To Make and Make Again*, 29.

5. The Politics of Women's Ritualizing

1. Despite contemporary reservations about the cultural imperialism of reading into ceremonies meanings unrecognized by their participants, other voices— from Amnesty International to Bruce Lincoln—demand that some standards of common morality inform our analysis of the ritual behavior of others. The latter discusses the case of female genital mutilation, concluding that no matter how well constructed and symbolically coherent such practices may be, they are ultimately systems for enforcing the domination of the powerful at the expense of the weak (even when the initiates themselves justify and desire the procedure) and thus are inherently immoral. See, for example, Lincoln, *Discourse*, 112–13.

2. Drewal, *Yoruba Ritual*, 174.

3. See Lawrence Hoffman (*Beyond the Text: A Holistic Approach to Liturgy* [Bloomington: Indiana University Press, 1988], 158) for an intriguing discussion of what he terms "censoring in" and "censoring out"—the need for new religions to protect their unique identity while at the same time establishing themselves within society's broad definition of religious acceptability. Although these concepts are not directly applicable to the problem of constitutive ritual, they do point to ritual's two-pronged definitive function as both internal and external.

4. Gerard A. Pottebaum, *The Rites of People: Exploring the Ritual Character of Human Experience* (Washington, D.C.: Pastoral Press, 1992), 109.

5. Ibid.

6. Kertzer, *Ritual, Politics, and Power*, 10.

7. Ibid., 6.

8. See Bruce Lincoln, *Emerging from the Chrysalis: Rituals of Women's Initiation* (New York: Oxford University Press, 1991), 118.

9. Bell, *Ritual Theory, Ritual Practice*, 130. Henry Pernet describes the latter function when discussing the masking rituals of men's secret societies in Africa, Melanesia, and America. Pernet argues that in masking societies, women are not at all frightened by the use of the mask (which they often have helped to prepare); rather, they are participants in a complex system of pseudosecrets that establishes group identities and roles and "authorize[s] manipulations enabling certain subgroups to secure the power for themselves" (*Ritual Masks*, 150). Rosalind I. J. Hackett suggests that in tolerating conventional displays of male domination, such as masking ceremonies, women actually gain ideological freedom ("Women in African Religions," in Sharma, *Religion and Women*, 82).

10. Lincoln, *Discourse*, 75.

11. Bell, *Ritual Theory, Ritual Practice*, 116.

12. Procter-Smith, *Praying with Our Eyes Open*, 65.

13. Chris Smith, "Feminist Spirituality," *Well Springs: A Journal of United Methodist Clergywomen* 3, no. 1 (spring 1990): 10.

14. Saul Alinsky, *Rules for Radicals: A Practical Primer for Realistic Radicals* (New York: Vintage Books, 1972), 50.

15. Lincoln, *Discourse*, 3, 4–5.

16. Pernet, *Ritual Masks*, 155.

17. Bell, *Ritual Theory, Ritual Practice*, 170.

18. See ibid., 171–74, for a summary of the work of these and other theorists.

19. Lincoln, *Discourse*, 4.

20. Ibid., 5.

21. Ibid., 8.

22. Ibid., 174.

23. Grimes, *Ritual Criticism*, 21.

24. Victor Turner, *Dramas, Fields, and Metaphors: Symbolic Action in Human Society* (Ithaca: Cornell University Press, 1974), 55.

25. For a further analysis of Turner's work in this regard, see David Raybin, "Aesthetics, Romance, and Turner," in *Victor Turner and the Construction of Cultural Criticism: Between Literature and Anthropology*, ed. Kathleen M. Ashley (Bloomington: Indiana University Press, 1990), 22–27.

Interestingly, despite Turner's views on ritual as an agent of change, he was a reactionary critic of the liturgical reforms of Vatican II, sounding much like any other aging churchgoer nostalgic for the familiar. See Victor Turner, "Ritual, Tribal and Catholic," *Worship* 50 (1976): 504–24.

26. Bell, "Authority of Ritual Experts," 117.

27. Ibid., 120.

28. Ibid., 117.

29. Roof, "Changing American Religious Landscape," 19.

30. Hoffman, *Beyond the Text*, 72.

31. Martha Ellen Stortz, "Ritual Power, Ritual Authority: Configurations and Reconfigurations in the Era of Manifestations," in Aune and DeMarinis, *Religious and Social Ritual*, 122.

32. Kertzer, *Ritual, Politics, and Power*, 87.

33. Sered, *Priestess, Mother, Sacred Sister*, 269–72.

34. Procter-Smith, "In the Line," 25.

35. Kertzer, *Ritual, Politics, and Power*, 181.

36. Vincie, "Gender Analysis and Christian Initiation," 529.

37. Maria Mies, "Women's Research or Feminist Research? The Debate surrounding Feminist Science and Methodology," in *Beyond Methodology: Feminist Scholarship as Lived Research*, ed. Mary Margaret Fonow and Judith A. Cook (Bloomington: Indiana University Press, 1991), 76.

38. Eko Susan Noble, "Eastern Traditions in Western Lands," in Tsomo, *Buddhism through American Women's Eyes*, 150.

39. Sered, *Priestess, Mother, Sacred Sister*, 269.

40. Raybin, "Aesthetics, Romance, and Turner," 27.

41. Hoffman, *Beyond the Text*, 75.

42. Kertzer, *Ritual, Politics, and Power*, 44.

43. Stortz, "Ritual Power, Ritual Authority," 122.

44. Driver, *Magic of Ritual*, 236.

45. Drewal, *Yoruba Ritual*, 171.

46. Lawrence A. Babb, *Redemptive Encounters: Three Modern Styles in the Hindu Tradition* (Berkeley: University of California Press, 1986), 96.

47. Sered, *Priestess, Mother, Sacred Sister*, 258.

48. Michael B. Aune, "Introductory Essay," in Aune and DeMarinis, *Religious and Social Ritual*, 142–43.

49. Ibid.

50. Lincoln, *Discourse*, 7.

51. Kertzer, *Ritual, Politics, and Power*, 92.

52. Lincoln, *Discourse*, 25.

53. Bell, *Ritual Theory, Ritual Practice*, 71.

54. Brown, *Mama Lola*, 55.

55. Forman, *Taking Our Time*, xiv.

56. Pernet, *Ritual Masks*, 152.

57. Eller, "Women's Religion," 190.

58. Procter-Smith, *Praying with Our Eyes Open*, 9.

59. Ibid., 12.

60. Ibid., 41.

61. Daly, *Beyond God the Father*, 40.

62. Serene Jones, response to "Emerging Patterns in Women's Ritualizing," by Lesley A. Northup (paper presented at Yale University Institute of Sacred Music, November 1995).

63. Ozorak, "Social Construction."

64. Wendy Doniger, "The Implied Spider: Politics and Theology in Myth," *Religious Studies News*, February 1997, 9.

65. Grey, "Method in Feminist Theology," 101.

66. Sered, *Priestess, Mother, Sacred Sister*, 254.

67. Stortz, "Ritual Power, Ritual Authority," 133.

6. The Future of Women's Ritualizing

1. Driver, *Magic of Ritual*, 92.

2. Ibid., 117.

3. See, for example, ibid., 91; Grimes, *Ritual Criticism*, 24–27; and Lincoln, *Discourse and the Construction of Society*, 75.

4. Vincie, "Rethinking Initiation Rituals," 159.

5. Kay Turner, "Contemporary Feminist Rituals," 229.

6. Tom Bremer, "Sacrificial Slaughter and Dressing Up: Gender Articulations in Muslim Rituals," *Religious Studies Review* 22, no. 3 (July 1996): 209.

7. Driver, *Magic of Ritual*, 46.

8. Neu, "Women Revisioning Religious Rituals," 155–72.

9. Films and novels seem to outpace scholarship in portraying women's community rituals. In addition to *How to Make an American Quilt*, movies such as *The Joy Luck Club, Steel Magnolias*, and *A League of Their Own* have explored the particularly ritual nature of women's gatherings.

10. Hoffman, *Beyond the Text*, 144.

11. Ibid., 76.

12. See, for example, Grimes, *Ritual Criticism*, 16.

13. Ibid., 18.

14. Fonow and Cook, *Beyond Methodology*, 2.

15. Frederick Turner, "'Hyperion to a Satyr': Criticism and Anti-structure in the Work of Victor Turner," in Ashley, *Victor Turner*, 149. Turner's model uses the metaphor of a frontier plain, over which students and scholars are spread in roughly equal numbers and in which experts toil relatively oblivious to all but the research most closely related to their own; to protect their turf, these experts develop arcane jargon available to others only after "humiliating

and protracted ordeals" (149). His description should be familiar to anyone in academia.

16. Eric Hobsbawm, "Introduction: Inventing Tradition," in *The Invention of Tradition,* ed. Hobsbawm and Terence Ranger (Cambridge: Cambridge University Press, 1983), 1.

17. Ibid., 4, 6. See also Grimes, *Reading, Writing, and Ritualizing,* 5, 30. Grimes suggests that new traditions are not "created whole cloth but that the incubating of new rites utilizes a nest of old 'parts' from dismembered older rites." He singles out feminist ritualizing as an example: "Though feminist ritual draws on traditional resources, much of it is the result of spontaneous improvisation and imaginative effort" (5).

18. Hobsbawm, "Introduction," 4–5.

19. Bell, *Ritual Theory, Ritual Practice,* 124.

20. Grimes, *Reading, Writing, and Ritualizing,* 30. Unlike Grimes, I do not understand Hobsbawm to say that invented traditions "are effective only if ritualists are self-deceived" (Grimes, *Reading, Writing, and Ritualizing,* 10). Rather Hobsbawm's point seems to me to be that where traditions are vital, meaningful, and vibrant, there is little need for new practices; it is where the old rituals fail to adapt and reflect newer realities that the creative impulse naturally turns to inventing new patterns.

21. Grimes, *Reading, Writing, and Ritualizing,* 31.

22. Hoffman, *Beyond the Text,* 78.

23. Bell, *Ritual Theory, Ritual Practice,* 69.

24. Aune, "Introductory Essay," 9.

25. Grimes, *Ritual Criticism,* 25. Even further, this postmodern consciousness implies the nonexistence of ritual altogether—a place where this book cannot go.

26. Ibid., 26.

27. Bell, *Ritual Theory, Ritual Practice,* 38.

28. Grimes, *Ritual Criticism,* 24.

29. See, for example, Jonathan Z. Smith, *Imagining Religion: From Babylon to Jonestown* (Chicago: University of Chicago Press, 1982); and Talal Asad, *Genealogies of Religion: Discipline and Reasons of Power in Christianity and Islam* (Baltimore: Johns Hopkins Press, 1993). Smith's suggestion that "religion" is a product of the imagination of scholars, presumably created ex nihilo simply to give scholars something about which to write, carries with it the irony that Smith's own critique would seem to be susceptible to the same logic. What more creative a scholarly enterprise could there be than to invent a whole new category of antischolarship to occupy the next wave of academics?

30. Catherine Bell, "Modernism and Postmodernism in the Study of Religion," *Religious Studies Review* 22, no. 3 (July 1996): 185.

31. Fulkerson, *Changing the Subject,* 16.

32. Bell, "Modernism and Postmodernism," 188.

33. Jane Lewis, "Women's History," 158.

34. Jane Caputi, "On Psychic Activism: Feminist Mythmaking," in Larrington, *The Feminist Companion to Mythology*, 435.

35. Fulkerson, *Changing the Subject*, 3.

36. Margaret Mary Kelleher, "Hermeneutics in the Study of Liturgical Performance," *Worship* 67, no. 4 (July 1993): 299.

37. Grimes, *Reading, Writing, and Ritualizing*, 19.

38. Ibid., 20–22.

39. As Grimes points out (ibid., 19), Victor Turner's work incorporated an operational category of meaning as well as an exegetical function.

40. Ibid., 37.

41. See S. R. Skees, "Pulling Down God from the Sky: Women-Church," *Witness* 77, nos. 8/9 (August/September 1994): 20.

42. Sered, *Priestess, Mother, Sacred Sister*, 195.

43. Peter Steinfels, "Beliefs," *New York Times*, 1 May 1993.

44. Christ and Plaskow, "Introduction," 9.

45. Eller, "Women's Religion," 174.

46. Bell, *Ritual Theory, Ritual Practice*, 210.

47. Kertzer, *Ritual, Politics, and Power*, 175.

48. Stein, *Casting the Circle*, 20.

49. Slough, "'Let Every Tongue,'" 180.

50. Lincoln, *Discourse*, 85.

51. Caron, *To Make and Make Again*, 39.

52. Grimes, *Ritual Criticism*, 110, 111.

53. Kay Turner, "Contemporary Feminist Rituals," 230.

54. Grimes, *Reading, Writing, and Ritualizing*, 11.

55. Hoffman, *Beyond the Text*, 128.

56. Caron, *To Make and Make Again*, 168; Starhawk, *Truth or Dare*, 155.

57. Ann Braude, "The Perils of Passivity: Women's Leadership in Spiritualism and Christian Science," in Wessinger, *Women's Leadership*, 65.

58. Martin, "Introductory Essay," 33.

59. Grimes, *Ritual Criticism*, 193.

60. Grimes, *Reading, Writing, and Ritualizing*, 31.

61. Susan J. White, *Christian Worship and Technological Change* (Nashville: Abingdon, 1994), 34.

62. Procter-Smith, *Praying with Our Eyes Open*, 143.

63. Theresa Berger, "The Women's Movement," 62.

64. Kay Turner, "Contemporary Feminist Rituals," 227.

65. Bell, "Authority of Ritual Experts," 120.

66. Bell, *Ritual Theory, Ritual Practice*, 210.

67. Skees, "Pulling Down God from the Sky," 20.

68. Ruether, "Women-Church Movement," 207.

69. Ibid., 208.

70. Skees, "Pulling Down God from the Sky," 19.

71. Berger, "Women's Movement," 62.

72. Steinfels, "Beliefs."

73. Richard Schechner, "The Future of Ritual," *Journal of Ritual Studies* 1, no. 1 (winter 1987): 30.

74. Procter-Smith, *In Her Own Rite*, 36–58.

75. In *In Her Own Rite*, an important early exploration of feminist liturgy, Procter-Smith details the relationship of memory and imagination from both a feminist and a Christian perspective. Like Richard Schechner ("Future of Ritual"), she relates these factors directly to bodiliness: "Memories and experience of the female body are no longer either marginalized or negative, but central to a more complete understanding of God, self, and community" (50).

76. Schechner, "Future of Ritual," 30.

Adams, William Seth. "An Apology for Variable Liturgical Space." *Worship* 61, no. 3 (May 1987): 231–42.

Andersson, Anne R. "Dismantling Patriarchy—A Redemptive Vision: Ritual and Feminist Critical Theology in Basic Ecclesial Communities" (1993). In Northup, 183–201.

Arnold, Marigene. "Célibes, Mothers, and Church Cockroaches" (1978). In Hoch-Smith and Spring, 45–53.

Ashley, Kathleen M., ed. *Victor Turner and the Construction of Cultural Criticism: Between Literature and Anthropology.* Bloomington: Indiana University Press, 1990.

Aune, Michael B., and Valerie DeMarinis, eds. *Religious and Social Ritual: Interdisciplinary Explorations.* Albany: State University of New York Press, 1996.

Babb, Lawrence A. *Redemptive Encounters: Three Modern Styles in the Hindu Tradition.* Berkeley: University of California Press, 1986.

Bednarowski, Mary Farrell. "Widening the Banks of the Mainstream: Women Constructing Theologies" (1993). In Wessinger, 211–31.

Bell, Catherine. "The Authority of Ritual Experts." *Studia Liturgica* 23, no. 1 (1993): 98–120.

———. "Modernism and Postmodernism in the Study of Religion." *Religious Studies Review* 22, no. 3 (July 1996): 179–90.

———. *Ritual Theory, Ritual Practice.* New York: Oxford University Press, 1992.

Berger, Theresa. "The Women's Movement as a Liturgical Movement: A Form of Inculturation?" *Studia Liturgica* 20, no. 1 (July 1990): 55–64.

Braude, Ann. "The Perils of Passivity: Women's Leadership in Spiritualism and Christian Science" (1993). In Wessinger, 55–67.

Bremer, Tom. "Sacrificial Slaughter and Dressing Up: Gender Articulations in Muslim Rituals." *Religious Studies Review* 22, no. 3 (July 1996): 209–13.

Brown, Karen McCarthy. *Mama Lola: A Vodou Priestess in Brooklyn.* Berkeley: University of California Press, 1991.

Bynum, Caroline Walker. "The Complexity of Symbols." In *Gender and Religion: On the Complexity of Symbols,* edited by Caroline Walker Bynum, Stevan Harrell, and Paula Richman, 1–20. Boston: Beacon, 1986.

Campo, Juan Eduardo. *The Other Sides of Paradise: Explorations into the Religious Meanings of Domestic Space in Islam.* Columbia: University of South Carolina Press, 1991.

Caputi, Jane. "On Psychic Activism: Feminist Mythmaking" (1992). In Larrington, 425–40.

Caron, Charlotte. *To Make and Make Again: Feminist Ritual Thealogy.* New York: Crossroad, 1993.

Christ, Carol P., and Judith Plaskow. "Introduction: Womanspirit Rising" (1979). In Christ and Plaskow, *Womanspirit Rising,* 1–17.

———, eds. *Womanspirit Rising: A Feminist Reader in Religion.* San Francisco: HarperSanFrancisco, 1979.

Collins, Mary. "An Adventuresome Hypothesis: Women as Authors of Liturgical Change." In *Proceedings of the North American Academy of Liturgy* (1993), 37–57.

———. "Principles of Feminist Liturgy" (1993). In Procter-Smith and Walton, 9–26.

Costen, Melva Wilson. "African-American Women and Religious Ritual" (1993). In Northup, 3–18.

Crites, Stephen. "Angels We Have Heard" (1975). In Wiggins, 23–64.

Daly, Mary. *The Church and the Second Sex: With the Feminist Postchristian Introduction and the New Archaic Afterwords.* Boston: Beacon, 1985.

———. "Original Reintroduction." In *Beyond God the Father: Toward a Philosophy of Women's Liberation.* Boston: Beacon, 1985.

Daly, Mary, with Jane Caputi. *Webster's First New Intergalactic Wickedary of the English Language.* San Francisco: HarperSanFrancisco, 1987.

Debuyst, Frédéric. "The Church, a Dwelling Place of Faith." *Studia Liturgica* 24, no. 1 (1994): 29–44.

Dijk, Denise J. J. "Developments in Feminist Liturgy in the Netherlands." *Studia Liturgica* 25, no. 1 (1995): 120–28.

Doniger, Wendy. "The Implied Spider: Politics and Theology in Myth." *Religious Studies News,* February 1997, 9.

Doty, William G. "The Stories of Our Times" (1975). In Wiggins, 93–121.

Drewal, Margaret Thompson. *Yoruba Ritual: Performers, Play, Agency.* Bloomington: Indiana University Press, 1992.

Driver, Tom F. *The Magic of Ritual: Our Need for Rites That Transform Our Lives and Our Communities.* San Francisco: HarperSanFrancisco, 1991.

Dugan, Kathleen M. "In the Beginning Was Woman: Women in Native American Religious Traditions" (1994). In Sharma, 39–60.

Eliade, Mircea. *The Sacred and the Profane.* Translated by Willard R. Trask. New York: Harcourt, Brace and Company, 1959.

Elkins, Heather Murray. *Worshiping Women: Re-forming God's People for Praise.* Nashville: Abingdon, 1994.

Eller, Cynthia. "Twentieth-Century Women's Religion as Seen in the Feminist Spirituality Movement" (1993). In Wessinger, 172–95.

Ellwood, Robert, and Catherine Wessinger. "The Feminism of 'Universal Brotherhood': Women in the Theosophical Movement" (1993). In Wessinger, 68–87.

Elwell, Sue Levi. "Reclaiming Jewish Women's Oral Tradition? An Analysis of Rosh Hodesh" (1993). In Procter-Smith and Walton, 111–26.

Erickson, Victoria Lee. "Victoria Lee Erickson Replies." *Journal of Feminist Studies in Religion* 10, no. 1 (spring 1994): 118–21.

Ermarth, Elizabeth Deeds. "The Solitude of Women and Social Time" (1989). In Forman, 37–46.

Estes, David C. "Ritual Validations of Clergywomen's Authority in the African American Spiritual Churches of New Orleans" (1993). In Wessinger, 149–71.

Falk, Nancy Auer, and Rita M. Gross, eds. *Unspoken Worlds: Women's Religious Lives.* Belmont, Calif.: Wadsworth, 1989.

Ferguson, Marianne. *Women and Religion.* Englewood Cliffs, N.J.: Prentice Hall, 1995.

Fonow, Mary Margaret, and Judith A. Cook. *Beyond Methodology: Feminist Scholarship as Lived Research.* Bloomington: Indiana University Press, 1991.

Forman, Frieda Johles, ed., with Caoran Sowton. *Taking Our Time: Feminist Perspectives on Temporality.* Athene Series. Elmsford, N.Y.: Pergamon, 1989.

Fulkerson, Mary McClintock. *Changing the Subject: Women's Discourses and Feminist Theology.* Minneapolis: Fortress, 1994.

Garcia, Irma. "Femalear Explorations: Temporality in Women's Writing." Translated by Eva Goliger Reisman (1989). In Forman, 161–82.

Glendinning, Chellis. "The Healing Powers of Women" (1982). In Spretnak, 280–93.

Gollin, Gillian Lindt. *Moravians in Two Worlds: A Study of Changing Communities.* New York: Columbia University Press, 1967.

Göttner-Abendroth, Heide. "Urania—Time and Space of the Stars: The Macrocosmal Cosmos through the Lens of Modern Physics" (1989). In Forman, 108–19.

Goudey, June C. "Worship and Gender: Toward Liturgies of Care." In *Proceedings of the North American Academy of Liturgy* (1993), 89–107.

Grey, Mary. "Method in Feminist Theology." *Feminist Theology*, no. 6 (May 1994): 90–102.

Grimes, Ronald L. *Beginnings in Ritual Studies*. Washington, D.C.: University Press of America, 1982.

———. "Liturgical Supinity, Liturgical Erectitude: On the Embodiment of Ritual Authority." *Studia Liturgica* 23, no. 1 (1993): 39–60.

———. *Reading, Writing, and Ritualizing: Ritual in Fictive, Liturgical, and Public Places*. Washington, D.C.: Pastoral Press, 1993.

———. *Ritual Criticism: Case Studies in Its Practice, Essays on Its Theory*. Columbia: University of South Carolina Press, 1990.

Hackett, Rosalind I. J. "Women in African Religions." In Sharma, 61–92.

Hall, Edward T. *The Hidden Dimension*. Garden City, N.Y.: Doubleday, Anchor, 1969.

Harris, Maria. *Dance of the Spirit: The Seven Steps of Women's Spirituality*. New York: Bantam, 1989.

Harrison, Beverly, in the Mud Flower Collective. *God's Fierce Whimsy: Christian Feminism and Theological Education*. New York: Pilgrim, 1985.

Harvey, Youngsook Kim. "Possession Sickness and Women Shamans in Korea" (1989). In Falk and Gross, 37–44.

Hewitt, Marsha Aileen. *Critical Theory of Religion: A Feminist Analysis*. Minneapolis: Fortress, 1995.

Hobsbawm, Eric. "Introduction: Inventing Tradition." In *The Invention of Tradition*, edited by Hobsbawm and Terence Ranger, 1–14. Cambridge: Cambridge University Press, 1983.

Hoch-Smith, Judith, and Anita Spring, eds. *Women in Ritual and Symbolic Roles*. New York: Plenum, 1978.

Hoffman, Lawrence. *Beyond the Text: A Holistic Approach to Liturgy*. Bloomington: Indiana University Press, 1988.

Jacobson, Doranne. "Golden Handprints and Red-Painted Feet: Hindu Childbirth Rituals in Central India" (1989). In Falk and Gross, 59–71.

Jones, Serene. Response to "Emerging Patterns in Women's Ritualizing," by Lesley A. Northup, paper presented at Yale University Institute of Sacred Music, November 1995.

Kahn, Robbie Pfeuffer. "Women and Time in Childbirth and during Lactation" (1989). In Forman, 20–36.

Kaminski, Phyllis H. "Claiming Our Voices: A Teaching/Learning Experiment." *Journal of Feminist Studies in Religion* 10, no. 1 (spring 1994): 123–42.

Kavanagh, Aidan. "Textuality and Deritualization: The Case of Western Liturgical Usage." *Studia Liturgica* 23, no. 1 (1993): 70–77.

Kelleher, Margaret Mary. "Hermeneutics in the Study of Liturgical Performance." *Worship* 67, no. 4 (July 1993): 292–318.

Kerns, Virginia. *Women and the Ancestors: Black Carib Kinship and Ritual.* Urbana: University of Illinois Press, 1989.

Kertzer, David. *Ritual, Politics, and Power.* New Haven: Yale University Press, 1988.

Keshgegian, Flora A. "Scripting the Self/Subjecting the Transcendent: Autobiography and Feminist Theology." Paper presented at the annual meeting of the American Academy of Religion, Chicago, Ill., November 1994.

King, Eileen. "A Lingering Question: What Is Feminist Prayer?" (1993). In Procter-Smith and Walton, 225–35.

Larrington, Carolyne, ed. *The Feminist Companion to Mythology.* London: Pandora, 1992.

Lawless, Elaine. "Not So Different a Story after All: Pentecostal Women in the Pulpit." In Wessinger, 41–54.

Levey, Michelle. "Everyday Dharma" (1995). In Tsomo, *Buddhism through American Women's Eyes,* 62–69.

Lewis, Jane. "Women's History, Gender History, and Feminist Politics." In *The Knowledge Explosion: Generations of Feminist Scholarship,* edited by Cheris Kramarae and Dale Spender, 154–60. New York: Teachers College Press.

Lincoln, Bruce. *Discourse and the Construction of Society: Comparative Studies of Myth, Ritual, and Classification.* New York: Oxford University Press, 1989.

———. *Emerging from the Chrysalis: Rituals of Women's Initiation.* New York: Oxford University Press, 1991.

Maitland, Sara. *A Map of the New Country: Women and Christianity.* London: Routledge & Kegan Paul, 1983.

Malarcher, Patricia. "Jubilee Ritual: A Creative Response" (1993). In Procter-Smith and Walton, 179–90.

Martin, John Hilary. "Introductory Essay" (1996). In Aune and DeMarinis, 19–47.

McDannell, Colleen. *The Christian Home in Victorian America, 1840–1900.* Bloomington: Indiana University Press, 1986.

McPhillips, Kath. "Women-Church and the Reclamation of Sacredness." *Journal of Feminist Studies in Religion* 10, no. 1 (spring 1994): 113–18.

McRobbie, Angela. "Dance and Social Fantasy." In *Gender and Generation,* edited by McRobbie and Mica Nava, 130–61. London: Macmillan, 1984.

Mernissi, Fatima. "Women, Saints, and Sanctuaries in Morocco" (1989). In Falk and Gross, 112–21.

Middleton-Keirn, Susan. "Convivial Sisterhood: Spirit Mediumship and Client-Core Network among Black South African Women" (1978). In Hoch-Smith and Spring, 191–205.

Mies, Maria. "Women's Research or Feminist Research? The Debate Surrounding Feminist Science and Methodology" (1991). In Fonow and Cook, 60–84.

Miller, Casey, and Kate Swift. *Words and Women: New Language in New Times*. Rev. ed. New York: HarperCollins, 1991.

Mitchell, Rosemary Catalano, and Gail Anderson Ricciuti. *Birthings and Blessings: Liberating Worship Services for the Inclusive Church*. New York: Crossroad, 1992.

Monroe, Irene. "The Aché Sisters: Discovering the Power of the Erotic in Ritual" (1993). In Procter-Smith and Walton, 127–35.

Myerhoff, Barbara G. "We Don't Wrap Herring in a Printed Page: Fusions, Fictions, and Continuity in Secular Ritual." In *Secular Ritual: Forms and Meanings*, edited by Sally F. Moore and Myerhoff, 112–38. Assen, Netherlands: Von Gorcum, 1977.

Neu, Dianne L. "Celebrating Women's Power." *WATERwheel* 6, no. 4 (winter 1993–94): 4–5.

———. "Examples and Ideas for Creating Feminist Rituals" (1993). In Neu and Hunt, 22–23.

———. "Liturgical Life of Women-Church: Defining Our Terms" (1993). In Neu and Hunt, 14–16.

———. "Planning Feminist Liturgy/Ritual" (1993). In Neu and Hunt, 17–21.

———. "Women Revisioning Religious Rituals" (1993). In Northup, 155–72.

Neu, Dianne L., and Mary E. Hunt. *Women-Church Sourcebook*. Washington, D.C.: WATERworks, 1993.

Noble, Eko Susan. "Eastern Traditions in Western Lands" (1995). In Tsomo, *Buddhism through American Women's Eyes*, 149–54.

Northup, Lesley A. "Claiming Horizontal Space: Women's Religious Rituals." *Studia Liturgica* 25, no. 1 (1995): 86–102.

Northup, Lesley A., ed. *Women and Religious Ritual*. Washington, D.C.: Pastoral Press, 1993.

Novak, Michael. "'Story' and Experience" (1975). In Wiggins, 175–78.

O'Brien, Mary. "Periods" (1989). In Forman, 11–18.

Ochs, Carol. *Behind the Sex of God*. Boston: Beacon, 1977.

O'Connell, J. B. *Church Building and Furnishing: The Church's Way: A Study in Liturgical Law*. Notre Dame, Ind.: University of Notre Dame Press, 1955.

Ozorak, Elizabeth. "The Social Construction of Women's Religious Self." Paper presented at the annual meeting of the American Psychological Association, Toronto, August 1996.

Pernet, Henry. *Ritual Masks: Deceptions and Revelations*. Columbia: University of South Carolina Press, 1992.

Plaskow, Judith, and Carol P. Christ, eds. *Weaving the Visions: Patterns in Feminist Spirituality.* San Francisco: HarperSan Francisco, 1989.

Pottebaum, Gerard A. *The Rites of People: Exploring the Ritual Character of Human Experience.* Rev. ed. Washington, D.C.: Pastoral Press, 1992.

Powers, Marla N. *Oglala Women: Myth, Ritual, and Reality.* Chicago: University of Chicago Press, 1986.

Prell-Foldes, Riv-Ellen. "Coming of Age in Kelton: The Constraints on Gender Symbolism in Jewish Ritual." In Hoch-Smith and Spring, 75–99.

Procter-Smith, Marjorie. *In Her Own Rite: Constructing Feminist Liturgical Tradition.* Nashville: Abingdon, 1990.

———. "In the Line of the Female: Shakerism and Feminism" (1993). In Wessinger, 23–40.

———. "Liturgical Anamnesis." *Worship* 61, no. 5 (September 1987): 405–24.

———. "The Marks of Feminist Liturgy." In *Proceedings of the North American Academy of Liturgy* (1992), 69–75.

———. *Praying with Our Eyes Open.* Nashville: Abingdon, 1995.

Procter-Smith, Marjorie, and Janet R. Walton, eds. *Women at Worship: Interpretations of North American Diversity.* Louisville, Ky.: Westminster/John Knox, 1993.

Purkiss, Diane. "Women's Rewriting of Myth" (1992). In Larrington, 441–58.

Rabuzzi, Kathryn Allen. "Bodyworship: The Gender-Masquerade of Fashion, Beauty, and Style" (1993). In Northup, 127–40.

Rand, Yvonne. "Abortion: A Respectful Meeting Ground" (1995). In Tsomo, *Buddhism through American Women's Eyes*, 85–89.

Raybin, David. "Aesthetics, Romance, and Turner" (1990). In Ashley, 21–41.

Reed, Esther D. "Whither Postmodernism and Feminist Theology?" *Feminist Theology*, no. 6 (May 1994): 15–29.

Rees, Bridget. "Women Withdrawing." *The Way*, supp. 67 (spring 1990): 62–72.

Roach, Catherine. "Loving Mother Earth: Some Reservations." *Hypatia* 6, no. 1 (spring 1991): 46–50. Abridged version published in James E. Huchingson, *Religion and the Natural Sciences: The Range of Engagement* (Fort Worth, Tex.: Harcourt Brace Jovanovich, 1993), 396-99.

Roberts, Wendy Hunter. "In Her Name: Toward a Feminist Thealogy of Pagan Ritual" (1993). In Procter-Smith and Walton, 137–62.

Roof, Wade Clark. "The Changing American Religious Landscape: Implications for Ritual." In *Proceedings of the North American Academy of Liturgy* (1994).

Ruach 13, no. 2 (spring 1992).

Ruether, Rosemary Radford. *Women-Church: Theology and Practice.* San Francisco: Harper & Row, 1985.

————. "The Women-Church Movement in Contemporary Christianity" (1993). In Wessinger, 196–210.

St. Hilda Community. *Women Included.* London: SPCK, 1991.

Schechner, Richard. "The Future of Ritual." *Journal of Ritual Studies* 1, no. 1 (winter 1987): 5–33.

Schlesinger, Arthur M. Introduction to *Pioneer Women: Voices from the Kansas Frontier,* by Joanna L. Stratton. New York: Simon and Schuster, Touchstone, 1981.

Schüssler Fiorenza, Elisabeth. "Emerging Issues in Feminist Biblical Interpretation." In *Christian Feminism: Visions of a New Humanity,* edited by Judith L. Weidman, 33–54. San Francisco: Harper & Row, 1984.

————. *In Memory of Her: A Feminist Reconstruction of Christian Origins.* New York: Crossroad, 1984.

Schwebel, Horst. "Liturgical Space and Human Experience, Exemplified by the Issue of the 'Multi-Purpose' Church Building." *Studia Liturgica* 24, no. 1 (1994): 12–28.

Seid-Martin, Sue. "Rituals for Re-Imagining." *Theological Markings* 2, no. 2 (summer 1994): 19.

Sered, Susan Starr. *Priestess, Mother, Sacred Sister: Religions Dominated by Women.* New York: Oxford University Press, 1994.

————. *Women as Religious Experts: The Religious Lives of Elderly Jewish Women in Jerusalem.* New York: Oxford University Press, 1992.

Sexson, Linda. "Let Talking Snakes Lie: Sacrificing Stories." In *Paths to the Power of Myth,* edited by Daniel C. Noel, 134–56. New York: Crossroad, 1994.

Sharma, Arvind, ed. *Religion and Women.* Albany: State University of New York Press, 1994.

Skees, S. R. "Pulling Down God from the Sky: Women-Church." *Witness* 77, nos. 8/9 (August/September 1994): 18–20.

Slough, Rebecca J. "'Let Every Tongue, by Art Refined, Mingle Its Softest Notes with Mine': An Exploration of Hymn-Singing Events and Dimensions of Knowing" (1996). In Aune and DeMarinis, 175–206.

Smith, Chris. "Feminist Spirituality." *Well Springs: A Journal of United Methodist Clergywomen* 3, no. 1 (spring 1990): 4–12.

Spretnak, Charlene, ed. *The Politics of Women's Spirituality: Essays on the Rise of Spiritual Power within the Feminist Movement.* New York: Doubleday, Anchor, 1982.

Starhawk. "Ritual as Bonding, Action as Ritual" (1979). In Christ and Plaskow, *Womanspirit Rising,* 326–35.

————. *The Spiral Dance.* San Francisco: HarperSanFrancisco, 1979.

————. *Truth or Dare*. New York: Harper & Row, 1987.

Stein, Diane. *Casting the Circle*. Freedom, Calif.: Crossing, 1990.

Steinfels, Peter. "Beliefs." *New York Times*, 1 May 1993.

Stortz, Martha Ellen. "Ritual Power, Ritual Authority: Configurations and Reconfigurations in the Era of Manifestations" (1996). In Aune and DeMarinis, 105–35.

Streza, Liviu. "The Mystagogy of Sacred Space according to Orthodox Theology." *Studia Liturgica* 24, no. 1 (1994): 84–90.

Swidler, Arlene. *Sister Celebrations*. Philadelphia: Fortress, 1974.

Tsomo, Karma Lekshe, ed. *Buddhism through American Women's Eyes*. Ithaca, N.Y.: Snow Lion, 1995.

————. "Continuing the Conversation" (1995). In Tsomo, *Buddhism through American Women's Eyes*, 155–60.

Turner, Frederick. "'Hyperion to a Satyr': Criticism and Anti-structure in the Work of Victor Turner" (1990). In Ashley, 147–62.

Turner, Kay. "Contemporary Feminist Rituals" (1982). In Spretnak, 219–33.

————. "The Virgin of Sorrows Procession: Mothers, Movement, and Transformation." *Arche: Notes and Papers on Archaic Studies* 6 (1981): 71–92.

Vincie, Catherine. "Gender Analysis and Christian Initiation." *Worship* 69, no. 6 (November 1995): 505–30.

————. "Rethinking Initiation Rituals: Do Women and Men Do It the Same Way?" In *Proceedings of the North American Academy of Liturgy* (1995).

Wadley, Susan. "Hindu Women's Family and Household Rites in a North Indian Village" (1989). In Falk and Gross, 72–81.

Walker, Barbara. *Women's Rituals*. San Francisco: HarperSanFrancisco, 1990.

Wessinger, Catherine, ed. *Women's Leadership in Marginal Religions: Explorations outside the Mainstream*. Urbana: University of Illinois Press, 1993.

White, James F. "Liturgy and the Language of Space." *Worship* 52, no. 1 (January 1978): 57–66.

White, Susan J. *Christian Worship and Technological Change*. Nashville: Abingdon, 1994.

Wiggins, James B., ed. *Religion as Story*. Lanham, Md.: University Press of America, 1975.

Worgul, George S. *From Magic to Metaphor: A Validation of the Christian Sacraments*. New York: Paulist, 1980.

index index index index **index** *index inde*

Index